Teach a Child to Read in One Week

Fast Foolproof Fun for Little Ones

Dr Bonnie J Macmillan

readin1week

First published in Great Britain in 2018 by readin1week

Trade paperback ISBN 978-1-9999663-9-3

For Martin

Contents

Introduction

Congratulations on choosing to buy this book, and let me reassure you right away that you have made a wise decision. By teaching your child to read at an early stage you will dramatically increase your child's chance of an exceptionally bright and successful future!

Learning to read is likely to be THE most important skill your child will ever learn. Your child's success in learning to read will have profound effects on your child's emotional health and well-being, on your child's level of intelligence and on his or her future academic and career success.

And the best part? You are going to find that teaching a child to read is far easier than you might have expected. Whether your child has yet to go to school, or has already started, you need not worry. With the *Teach a Child to Read in One Week* game-by-game system, you can teach your child to read amazingly quickly and easily.

Recent advances in the fields of learning and memory, and in the neuroscience of reading mean that we now know better than ever before how best to teach any child to read. This means that for the first time, you now have in your hands an absolutely foolproof set of state-of-the-art, early reading games that will astound you with the fast results they bring.

Just why do these games work so well?

Fun

These games are fun. They are deliberately engineered to be that way for a reason. When a child is having fun his brain is flooded with positive hormones creating the optimal conditions for the maximum amount of learning to take place. Humour helps children to concentrate better and tire less easily.

All the games are specifically designed to be highly entertaining to children aged 3 to 8. The illustrated readers at the end of each chapter make children chuckle, and the amusing cartoon-like pictures and mini-stories that teach letter shapes and their sounds capture the attention of young children.

Fast

The *Teach a Child to Read in One Week* games teach children to read unusually quickly. No time is devoted to activities that are known to have little or no effect on learning to read.

In short, those practices not sufficiently supported by scientific evidence are excluded. This includes teaching children to recognize whole words, or to remember letter names or upper case letter shapes. Learning upper case letter shapes to begin with is unnecessary since more than 95% of print is written using lower case letters. Also excluded, children are not taught to hear the separate sounds in spoken words without the use of letters. Only in conjunction with letters of the alphabet does this kind of training have any effect on learning to read. There is no instruction in how to write letters, or trace their shapes, since evidence does not support this as an effective learning to read strategy. Instead, instruction concentrates exclusively on activities that have been shown to have measurable effects on learning to read.

Boosting your child's enthusiasm for continued game playing, instruction is sequenced in very small steps to ensure that your child simply *cannot fail* and consistently experiences the thrill of success. Rewards are integral to the games and operate to further accelerate learning. Just having a parent's undivided, one-on-one attention is the ultimate reward for young children. Whether it is your glowing praise, a hug or a kiss, or a small toy or snack, such rewards guarantee that your child will learn fast.

Foolproof

The instruction in this book is based on fast code-learning. Scientific research shows that an approach that systematically teaches letter-to-sound correspondences, first and fast, consistently leads to superior achievement in reading, spelling, phoneme awareness and reading comprehension. Furthermore, the long-term effects of such an approach can be startling: six years after initial training, children taught this way are able to read on average at a level *three and a half years above* what one would expect for their age.

Neuroscientific

Recent brain-imaging research has discovered that an early code approach is the best way to speed the growth of left-hemisphere neural networks needed for reading. These are the brain pathways that *all* people must develop if they are to read. In *Reading in the Brain*, Stanislas Dehaene describes in fascinating detail the recent advances in neuroscience that have important implications for early reading instruction.

We now know that during reading, the brain performs a sequence of steps. It's difficult for adults to remember what the brain once did because the processes involved become increasingly automatic.

However, imaging studies reveal exactly what happens. First, the sight of a printed word activates a region in the back of the brain that analyses visual stimuli (see diagram next page, #1).

Second, if the stimulus is a word, signals are sent to a second region where, *with the right kind of instruction*, the neural pathways in this region develop the greater precision needed to recognize letter shapes (#2).

In a third step, the brain networks in charge of speech and language are activated. *Instruction is required* for these networks to develop the crucial ability to translate letter shapes into speech sounds, as well as the ability to blend a series of speech sounds in a word together (#3).

Finally, networks in charge of understanding spoken words (#4) are activated in order to analyse the word's meaning. Such networks are already well developed before most children learn to read.

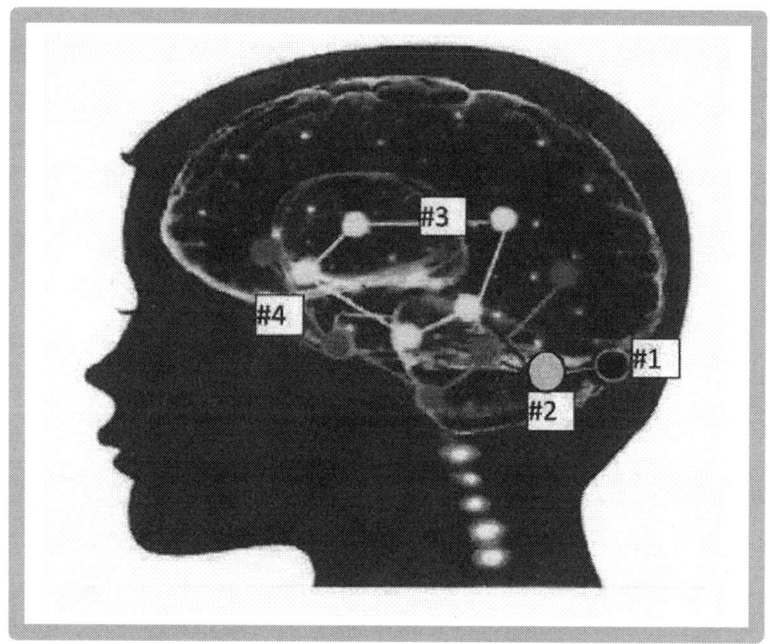

This picture shows the left side of the brain. During reading, it is regions and neural networks primarily on the left side of the brain that are activated.

Revolutionary letter-sound instruction

We are born neither with the ability to recognize letter shapes, nor the ability to translate letter shapes into speech sounds. These skills do not develop in the absence of instruction. Brain imaging research has demonstrated, however, how just a few hours of code-oriented instruction, teaching letter shapes and their associated sounds, can result in changes to both the anatomy and functioning of the brain.

The ability to remember letter shape and letter-sound information is absolutely *critical to learning to read.* But there is one problem. Letter-sound information is somewhat abstract, making it difficult for a young child to learn and remember. The key to effective instruction is in making this information more concrete and relatable to the minds of young children. This is the express purpose of the *Comic Mnemonics* (/ni-mon-icks/).

These memory-enhancing devices rely on evidence from learning, memory and brain research and aim to firmly 'fix' the essential letter-sound facts in your child's mind. Each mnemonic consists of a cartoon-type picture and an accompanying mini-story.

A number of factors make them potent memory-enhancing devices:

- First, while research shows that pictures are remembered better than words – known as the 'picture superiority effect', bizarre or humorous images are remembered even better. This is perhaps because they tend to illicit a greater number of eye fixations when they are viewed. The Comic Mnemonic pictures are unusual because although the abstract letter shapes have been altered slightly to resemble familiar objects, they also have surprising or amusing features.
- Second, letters are portrayed as little entities with their own human-type problems, worries, emotions and mishaps. When inanimate objects are given human characteristics, emotional centres in your child's brain are activated. Since there is a degree of overlap between the emotional centres and memory storage areas of the brain, these anthropomorphic-type pictures work to boost your child's memory for them even further.
- Third, and most important, when it comes to teaching letter-sound relations, evidence shows that only one type of picture works: the picture must closely link

the letter shape and letter-sound information. The *Comic Mnemonics* do this by explaining *why* a certain letter shape 'makes' or 'says' the sound that it does.

- Finally, the use of an accompanying mini-story to weave all the elements of the picture into an understandable whole operates not only to increase the number of eye fixations, and thus the time your child spends looking at the image, but also to enhance your child's comprehension and recall of it.

To illustrate, in the letter **a** picture, there are FOUR memory-boosting elements:

1) The letter is slightly altered to resemble an apple, something a child is likely to be familiar with, but *bizarrely*, this apple also has arms and legs

2) The apple, pictured falling from the tree, has an alarmed expression, a human characteristic likely to activate *emotional* centres in the brain of the viewer.

3) The apple-shaped letter is pictured screaming the sound 'aaa', immediately establishing a close *link between the letter shape and its sound.*

4) The accompanying *mini-story* explains and confirms why the apple shouts out this particular sound: it is frightened to be falling from the tree.

Bizarre, emotionally arousing, and closely linking a letter shape with its sound via a story, the Comic Mnemonics are potent memory- enhancing devices.

How to play the games

This instruction is designed to school-proof your child against reading problems. So it is best used *before* your child starts school and can be used from age 3 or even earlier. If your child has already started school and is exhibiting memorization or guessing behaviours, it is important to counteract them as soon as possible. The more you play the *Teach a Child to Read in One Week* games, the sooner you can help your child's brain grow and develop the correct neural pathways that underlie all fluent reading.

Your time-table can be flexible

Try to play the games for about 20 minutes a day. But, the length of your game-playing sessions will depend on how much time you have available, and your child's age and attention span. Feel free to proceed at either a faster or slower pace. If you miss a few days, just replay some of the games again. Keep in mind that your absolute top priority should be to have fun together.

No preparation time is required

All the materials needed to play the games can be found in this updated version of the book (January, 2020). The following materials are designed for easy removal from the book: 1) 'Comic Mnemonic Reminder' Cards (in the Appendix, at the end of the book) and 2) 'Lower Case Letter' Cards (pp. 21, 55, 101).

From the *Read Right Away* website, if you need them, you can download extra letter cards here: 45 LETTER CARDS (pdf)Download. If you are interested, you can make manipulative materials for some of the games. If you see a hand symbol next to the name of a game (✋), and you don't mind taking the time, you can download some additional materials here by clicking on this link: BOOK SUPPLEMENT FOR OPTIONAL USE (pdf)

Rewards are important

For the best results, you will need to reward your child. For the most part, you can do this via your enthusiastic praise, glowing compliments and lots of heartfelt hugs and kisses. Beyond that, you may wish to keep some special rewards on hand such as tiny snacks, stickers, balloons and so on. Please go ahead and get started with the games in Chapter 1 now. You are about to see your child sounding out and reading words within just ONE AMAZING WEEK!

Chapter 1

a s t n i p

Contents

Chapter 1

Welcome to Chapter 1 of *Teach a Child to Read in One Week*. Yes, it's true. In just one week, these extraordinarily powerful games will teach your child to:

1) Recognise these six letter shapes: **a**, **s**, **t** , **n**, **i** , **p**
2) Remember the *sounds* they represent: /a/ /s/ /t/ /n/ /i/ /p/
3) Blend two letter-sounds together to make a *new* sound
4) READ simple 3-letter words

To see this magic unfold, simply have fun playing these games with your child for 20 minutes a day. Yes it is possible to teach a child how to read in one week, but there is no pressure to complete the games in just one week. Depending on your child's age, and attention span, feel free to allow as little as 4 or 5 days and as long as 10 to 12 days. Above all, the main aim should be to have so much fun that your child will not want to stop playing these games with you!

Using the Comic Mnemonics (/ni-mon-icks/)

This chapter contains six unique Comic Mnemonics. Each of these consists of a bizarre picture and a mini-story. These state-of-the-art, memory-enhancing devices teach your child essential letter information, information that is fundamental to learning how to read. The pictures and the mini-stories are not just entertaining, it is the very explicit *links* they provide between a letter shape and its sound that make them so unusually effective.

Letter-shape: The pictures teach a child to associate the shape of a letter with something concrete they already know. As an example, a child is helped to remember the letter **a** shape because its shape resembles a round apple. But how can a child be helped to remember *what sound* that letter shape normally represents?

Letter-Sound: The concept of a letter's sound is even more abstract than a letter's shape. It is even more important that the story you tell your child about a letter's *sound* is something he or she can understand easily.

This is why the *Comic Mnemonic* pictures depict the letter shapes as small humanlike beings that 'talk'. Children understand that people talk, so they can easily grasp the concept that letters might talk too!

However, the *Comic Mnemonics* are unlike any sort of alphabet teaching tool. If alphabet books teach the *sounds* of letters at all, it happens only indirectly. Children are expected not only to hear the initial sound /a/ in the word pictured (antelope, axe, apple, or Annie), but also to deduce that the letter shape **a**, **a** or **A** represents the sound /a/. Studies consistently show, however, that young, non-reading children are simply incapable of hearing the initial sound in a spoken word. Nor are they able to understand, *without being told*, that a squiggly letter shape represents a sound. They need to be explicitly told what the initial sound in a word is. And they need to be directly told what a particular letter shape 'says' or 'makes'.

The amusing *Comic Mnemonic* pictures depict letter shapes 'making' their single, isolated sounds. These, along with the mini-stories, make it easy for children to remember what sound a letter 'says' because, importantly, they also *explain why* a certain letter shape 'makes' its particular sound.

Here is how to use the Comic Mnemonics:

- *Sequence*

  The Comic Mnemonics follow the letter sequence: **a s t n i p.** Simply display each of these mnemonics in turn and play *all five games,* Games 1 – 5, with each one.

- *How to read the stories*

  When you are reading the text that accompanies each picture, note that the letters which appear within slashes - /s/, indicate a *sound,* the sound associated with that letter. So you would pronounce/a/ like the initial sound heard in the word *apple*, /s/ like the initial sound heard in the word *snake*, and so on.

- *Avoid the /uh/ sound*

  When pronouncing letter-sounds try not to include an 'uh' sound (known as the schwa sound). Keep the sound short: /b/, not /buh/, /t/, not /tuh/, /p/, and not /puh/. Later, when your child learns how to blend letter-sounds together, it will be easier to arrive at the correct blended sound if you have been careful to avoid the /uh/ sound. In the word *sat,* for example, your child will find it easier to blend the three sounds together if he pronounces the sounds /s/ /a/ /t/, and *not:* /suh/ /a/ /t/.

- *Letter-sounds that continue*

  Some letter-sounds are known as *continuants.* When you pronounce these letter - sounds, the sound continues:

  The sound /f/ is pronounced 'ffffffff', not /fuh/

  The sound /l/ is pronounced 'llllllllll', not /luh/

  The sound /m/ is pronounced 'mmmmm', not /muh/

  The sound /n/ is pronounced 'nnnnnn', not /nuh/

  The sound /r/ is pronounces 'rrrrrrrr', not /ruh/

  The sound /s/ is pronounced 'sssssss', not /suh/

  The sound /v/ is pronounced 'vvvvvv', not /vuh/

  The sound /z/ is pronounced 'zzzzzzzz'; not /zuh/

- *Letter names*

  If your child already knows the *names* of letters, you may find that he comments, 'That's not a /sssss/. That's an /ess/.' Simply explain along these lines: 'Yes, you are right! That is the *name* of that letter. But when the letter *talks*, it doesn't say its name. It makes a *different* sound. It says /ssss/. Your name is (Max), but when you *talk*, you don't say, *Max, Max, Max,* ...., do you? You make different sounds.'

A Suggested 7-Day Plan

Day

1	Show your child each of the Comic Mnemonic pages in turn for the letters **a s t** (pp 11-13). Play Games 1- 5 with each one.
2	Show your child each of the Comic Mnemonic pages in turn for the letters **n i p** (pp 14-16). Play Games 1–5 with each one. Play Game 6.
3	Play Game 6 again. Play Games 7, 8, and 9.
4	Play Games 10, 11 and 12.
5	Play Games 13, 14, 15, and 16.
6	Play Games 17, 18, and 19.
7	Play Game 20, and Game 21, the *In A Spin* reader.

COMIC MNEMONIC GAMES

Step 1) Remove a 'Comic Mnemonic Reminder Card' from the Appendix.

Step 2) Display one of the Day 1 or 2 Comic Mnemonic pictures (pp 11-16).

Step 3) Play all Games 1-5 with your child while viewing each mnemonic picture.

Detailed instructions for Games 1 – 5 follow. However, when you examine a Comic Mnemonic picture together, you can refer to the 'Comic Mnemonic Reminder Card' to remind you how to play the five games.

Game 1 – Shifty Shapes

- Read the mini-story to your child. Read the mini-story again while you point out what is happening in the picture.
- Discuss the details of the letter *shape*. Ask, 'What does this letter look like?'
- Ask, 'Can you find another letter in the picture that looks the same?'
- Point to the text and ask, 'Can you find another /a/ (/s/, /t/, /n/, /i/, /p/) here?' (Be sure to say the *sound* of a letter, not its name).
- Point to various individual letter shapes in the picture and the text (not always the target letter), and ask *yes* or *no* questions about the target letter shape: 'Is this a /t/? Is this letter an /a/?' Praise your child's cleverness enthusiastically.

Game 2 – A Sound Story

- Read the story to your child once again. Then ask questions that focus on the letter's *sound* -
- 'What sound does the apple/snake/tower/Nora's mouth/ the insect/the parrot make/? What sound does it make again?'
- Ask WHY the letter makes a certain sound: The apple is scared, the snake sings along (point to its mouth) and makes a slip-sliding noise (point to its tail), a clock (point to it) in the tower ticks, Nora is naughty and makes an unpleasant sound, the insect makes a tiny little sound, and the parrot is proud and puffed up (point to its chest) and makes a puffing sound.
- Ask your child to make the letter's sound in different voices. For /a/, alarmed and frightened, for /s/, happy singing, for /t/, steady and mechanical, for /n/, sneering and unpleasant, for /i/, tiny and timid, for /p/, puffed up and proud. The aim is to have your child *say the sound* of the letter as many times as possible in response to looking at the letter's shape. Praise your child's efforts.

Game 3 – Talking Letters

- Read the story again. Focus on having your *child say the sound* of a letter while you point to it and describe its shape.

- Point to details in the *illustration* and ask, 'What does this big, fat apple-shaped letter say? What does it say again?'
- Point to the letters that appear in the *text*, and ask, 'What does this letter say? And, this one? And what about this letter?' Repeat many times.
- Point to letters other than the target letter to check that your child is not on 'automatic pilot'.
- Find examples of particular letter shapes while out shopping, on packaging or tins, and ask, 'Do you remember what this letter *says*?' Praise your child lavishly.

Game 4 - Let's Clown Around

- Read the story again but this time, you and your child can adopt the letter shapes, and act out the letter's character. Together, be as silly as you can be.
- Depending on the story, pretend to be:
  The fat apple falling off the tree, screaming with alarm, '/aaa/!'
  The snake, slipping and sliding, singing a hissing song, '/sssssss/!'
  The tower, standing rigid, tall and straight, steadily ticking, '/t / /t/ /t/.'
  Naughty Nora with her unpleasantly shaped mouth, taunting, '/n /, /n/ /n/' with her nasty, naughty continuous /nnnnnn/ sound.
  The tiny insect, lots of little legs (fingers) waving, squeaking, '/ i / -/i/ -/i/.'
  The parrot, with its proud, superior expression, puffing '/p/ / p/ / p/'.

Game 5 – Song and Dance Routine

- Give your child one of the chapter 1 letters. (Simply remove page 21 and cut out the lower case letter cards as needed.)
- Have your child compare the letter to the one in a Comic Mnemonic picture, and ask, 'Does this letter look the *same* as the one in this picture?'
- Ask, 'Can you put it the right way up, beside one that looks exactly the same?'
- Once your child does this correctly, it becomes the signal to begin the *Song and Dance* routine. Encourage your child to sing the mini-story with you to the nursery rhyme tune indicated while your child makes the letter dance around.

♫ *Ring around the roses*

/a/ looks like an apple

He's so big and fat and round

'/a/ - /a/!' - he shouts

As he falls down

♫ *Simple Simon*

Slinky Snaky spies a human

Standing in the sun

Sings Snaky '/sss/-/sss/, I can ssslip - ssslide

You can try - it's fun!'

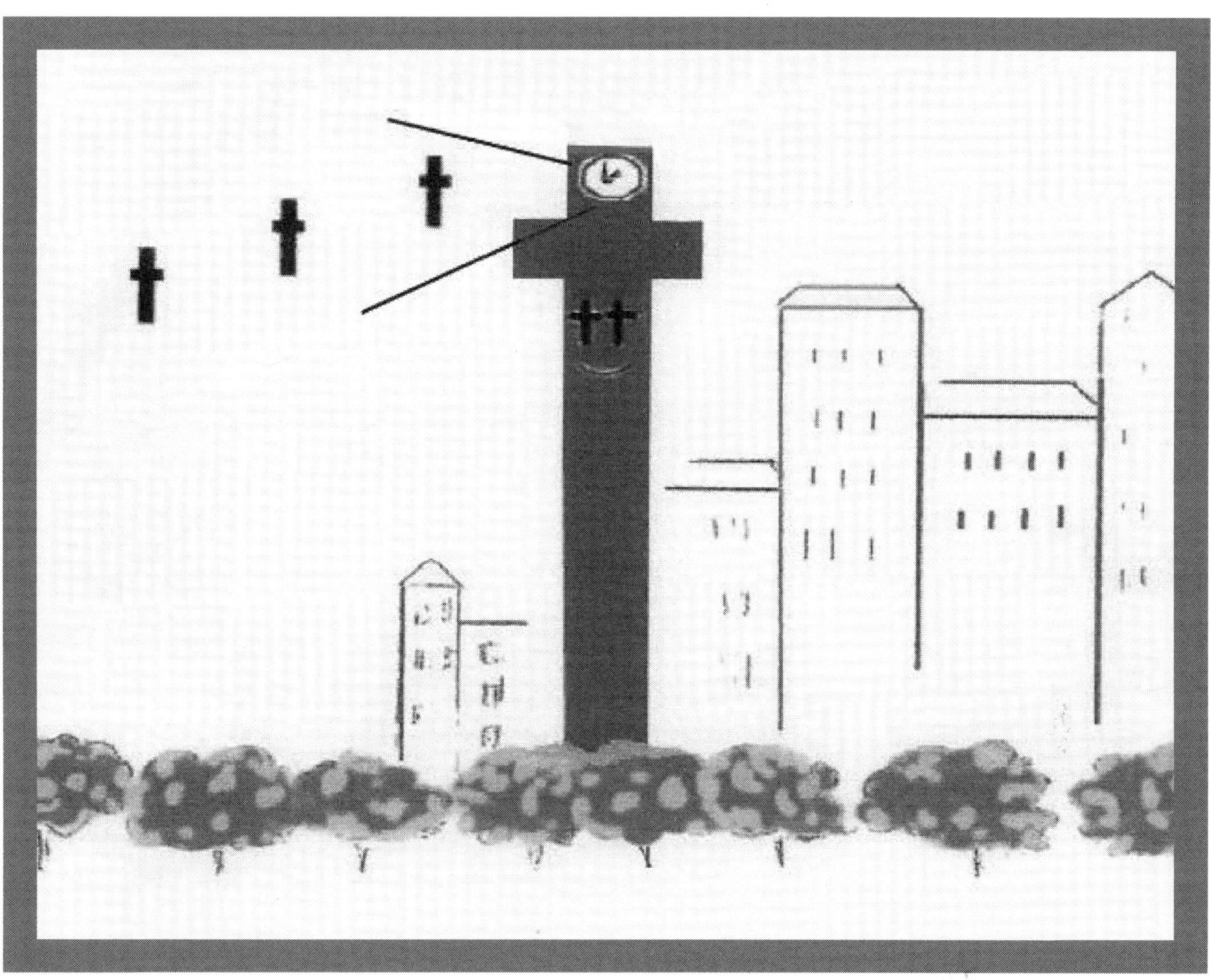

♫ *Hickory dickory dock*

Tickory
tickory
tock!
Like a clock tower high
/t/ touches the sky
Tick – or – y
/t/ - /t/ - /t/
tock!

♫ *Hey Diddle Diddle*

Look! Naughty Nora

Her mouth is drooping down

Hear her say, /n/ /n/, /n/ /n/

Not very nice – no, a nasty sound

/n/ /n/ /n/ /n/ /n-n/, /n/ /n/ /n/ !

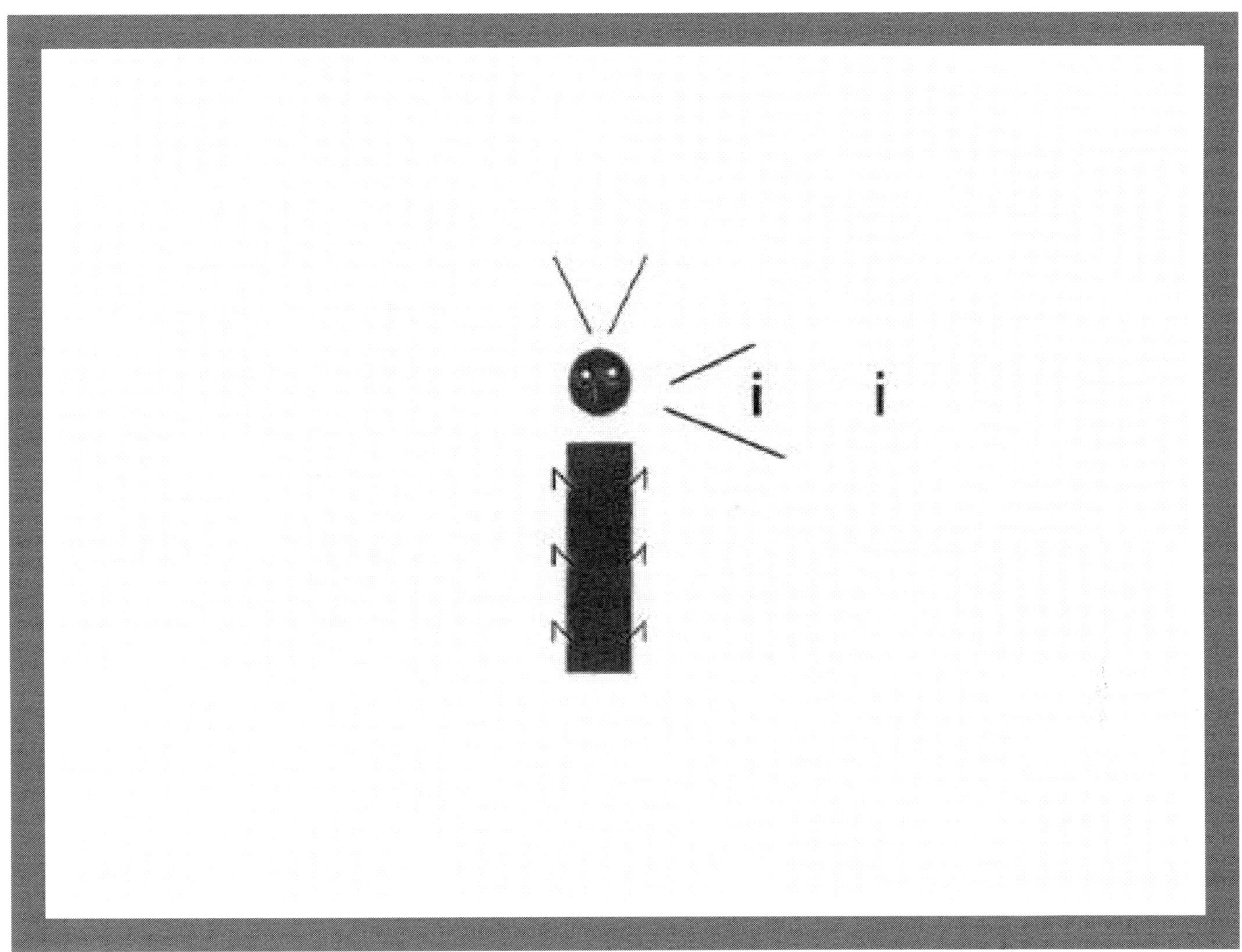

Incy Wincy Spider

Itsy bitsy insect
Tiny as can be
/i/ is itsy
'/i/ - /i/' he says
'it's me !'

♫ *I'm a LittleTeapot*

/p/ like a parakeet
Might he pop?
/p/ /p/ /p/ he puffs
Never does he stop
/p/ /p/ /p p/ /p/ /p/
Hear him puff!
Puffed up parrot
Thinks he's hot stuff

Game 6 – Tricky Pictures

PART ONE: Together, look at all the Comic Mnemonic pictures on pages 11 to 16.

- Ask lots of 'Can you find . . . ?' questions such as: 'Can you find a picture where the letter looks like a tall clock tower/a parrot /a tiny insect/ a wiggly snake/a round apple/Nora's upside-down mouth?'
- Point to various letters and ask, 'What does this letter say?'
- Point to letters and ask *why* questions about the sound a letter makes: 'Why does this letter say /t/, (/s/, /n/, /a/, /p/, /i/?' Give your child plenty of enthusiastic praise and lots of hugs.

PART TWO: Now show your child this page with its smaller pictures in the box above.

- Play the *Tricky Pictures* game again.

LICKETY-SPLIT LETTER-SOUND GAMES

Game 7 – Point and Shout

- Show your child this page. Say, 'The letters below are sleepy right now, but normally they like to talk a lot and make their special noise.'
- Say, 'Let's take turns to point at them and see if they make their sound.'
- Take turns pointing at random to a letter shape. The other player can then 'make' the letter's sound in a loud, excited voice.
- Later, see if your child can make all the letters talk proceeding from left to right, along all rows, from /a/ to /i/. If a mistake is made, the other player starts again and has a turn to make all the letters talk.

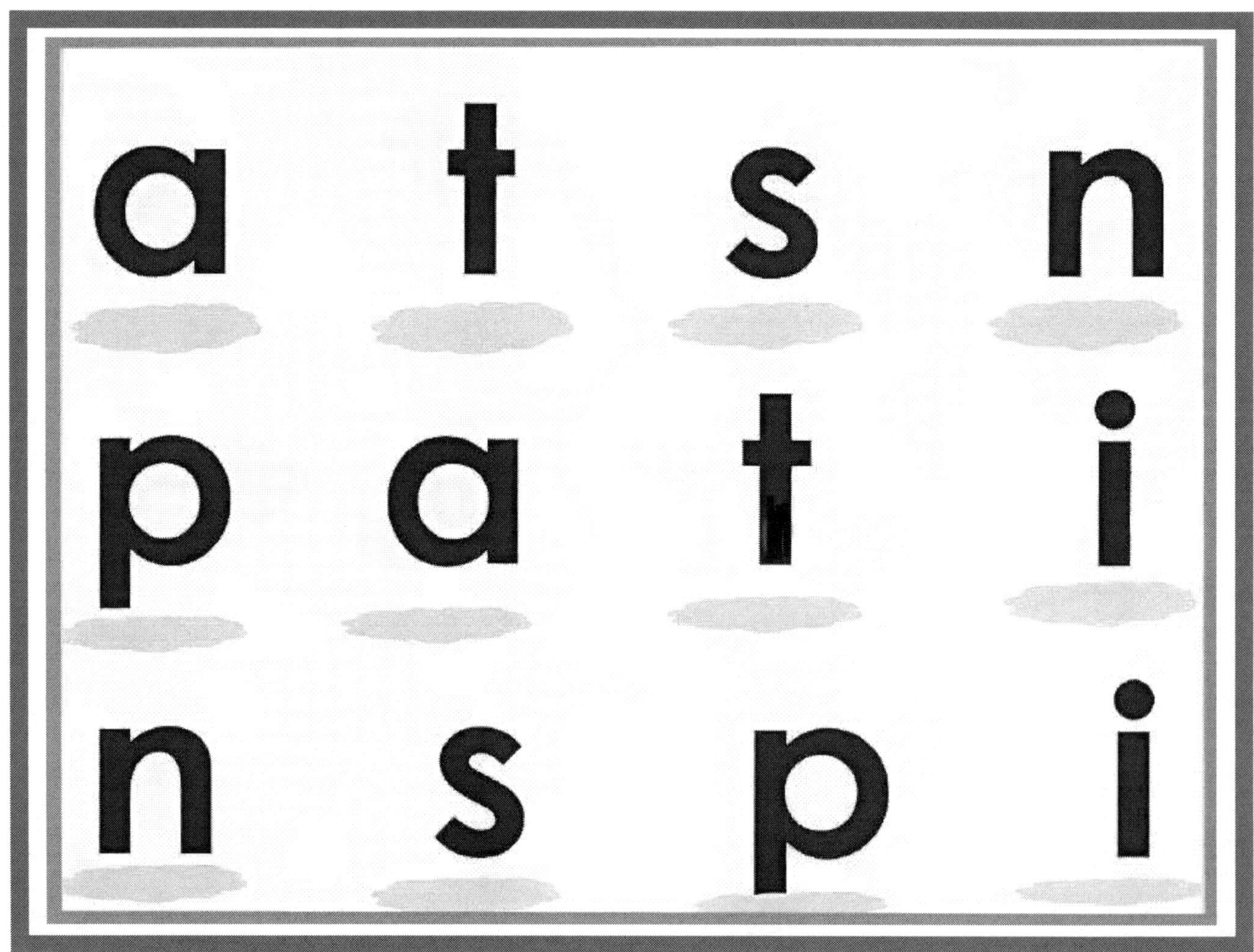

Game 8 – Fun and Games

s	t	a
n	i	p

1) Hunt the Letter

Direct attention to the letters above and ask, 'Can you find the letter that says ____________?

2) Make the Letters Talk

Point to the various letters and ask, 'When this letter talks, what does it say?'

3) Lookalike

Ask, 'Can you point to the letter that looks like:

- a puffed up parakeet?
- a big, fat apple?
- a slithery snake?
- naughty Nora's mouth?
- an itsy-bitsy insect?
- a tall tower?'
-

4) Match and Speak

Point to each letter below, and ask your child to find a letter above that looks the same. Can he tell you what it says?

n p i a s t

Game 9 – Lucky Dip

- Find the 'Lower Case Letter Cards' (p 21). Cut some up. Put them in a container.
- Say, 'The letters in here are all asleep. Shall we wake them up?'
- Take turns to choose a letter, say its sound, and put it down.
- When there are no more letters, the players scamper away with their collection of letters and hide them in plain sight somewhere.
- Then exclaim, 'Oh! It's time for the letters to go back to sleep!' Each player then looks for, and finds the letters *the other player* hid.
- As each letter is put 'back to bed' (in the container), players make them say *goodnight* by saying their sound.

Game 10 – The Treasure Hunt

- Select two sets of letter cards for the letters **a s t n i p**. Place the cards in a trail, inside the house or outdoors.
- At the end of the trail, hide a treasure your child will particularly like.
- Invite your child, 'Would you like to go on a treasure hunt?
- Show him where the treasure hunt starts, the first letter on the trail.
- Ask, 'What does this first clue say?' Pretend to be hard of hearing as a ploy to have your child repeat the letter's sound and pronounce it louder.
- Encourage your child to find more clues until he reaches the end of the trail and finds the treasure, an item he will particularly like.

Lower Case Letter Cards

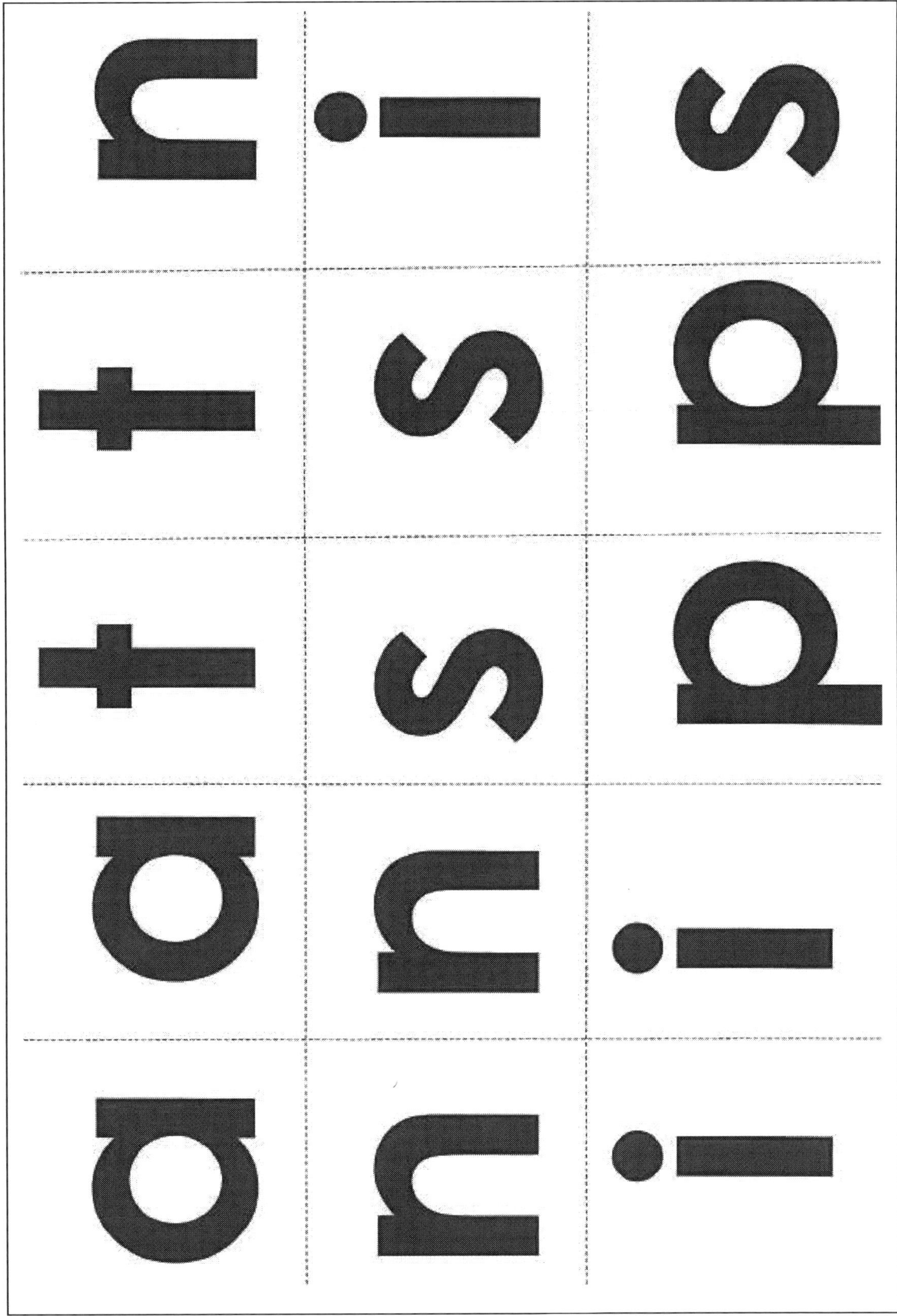

Left intentionally blank for Lower Case Letter Cards on reverse

MIND-BENDING SOUND BLENDING

Game 11 – Let's Get Together!

- Select the following four letter cards: **s, n, a, i** .

- Tell your child this story with actions: Hold up the **a** card, and say, 'Oh, look at me! I'm a letter. I say /a/.'
- Give your child the **n** card, and continue, 'And look at you! You're a letter too! And what do *you* say?' (Child says, '/nnn/'.)

- Now say, 'I can say /a/, but I can *only* say /a/.' Make a sad face.

- Ask, 'You can say?' (/n/) 'But you can *only* say /n/. Right?'
- Explain, 'This is why letters like to get together. When letters get together, they can make NEW sounds.'
- Ask, 'I wonder what would happen if *we* got *our* two letters together?'

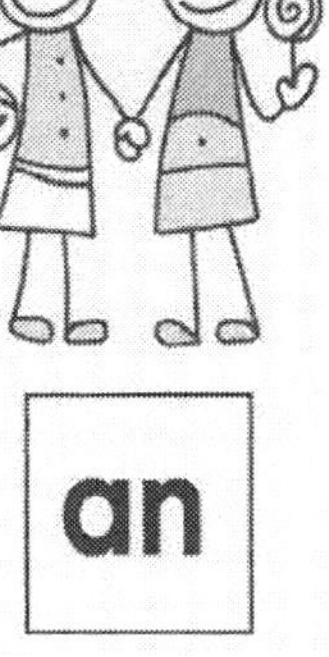

- Push your two letters together so that they are side by side as shown.

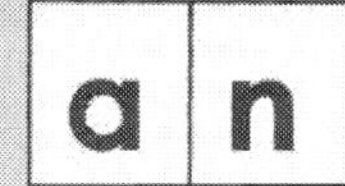

- Point underneath the letter **a**, and together say /a/, stretching the /a/ sound out in one continuous long sound.
- Then, *pointing underneath the letter* **n**, *run* the /a/ sound into the /n/ sound. Repeat this over and over together with your child joining in:
  '/aaa/ . . . n/; /aaa/. . . /n/; /aaa/ . . . /n/'.
- Then exclaim, '/an/!' Ask, 'Is the new sound? *an*?'
- Ask, 'Can *you* make that NEW sound? Again? Louder? Congratulate with enthusiasm.

Game 12 – Together and Apart

an in na ni sa si

Select the following letter cards and put them in a pile: **s, n, a, i**.

- Players choose a letter to make one of the letter pairs above.
- Can they push their letters together side by side to make one of the six letter pairs shown above?
- If so, both players sound and lengthen the first sound together, slide it into the second sound, and say the new sound.

- For example: '/aaa/ ....../n/', '/a/.../n/', '/an/'.
- Next, the players move their two letters *apart* and take turns to pronounce the two sounds *separately* as follows: Player A says: '/a/'. Player B says, '/n/'.
- Repeat the game with 2 new letters.

Game 13 – Birds in the Bush

On the next page, put some tiny treats that your child will enjoy on the circles under the 'bushes' to represent 'seeds'. Explain, 'In this game, you are a hungry bird looking for tasty seeds.'

- Now point to the first line where there are two 'bushes': one that says /sa/ (heard at the start of the word *sat*), and one, that says /si/ (as heard at the start of the word *sit*).
- Ask, 'Which one of these 2 bushes says /sa/ (/si/)/?' If your child points to the correct bush, he snaps up the 'seed'. If not, the 'seed' is left in place, and you move on to ask about other bushes. When you stop playing, any 'seeds' that have not been eaten, will be swallowed by a big, hungry 'crow' that happens to come by (i.e. YOU)!
- Play the game until your little 'bird' becomes clever enough not to leave any seeds behind for the crow.

Game 13 – Birds in the Bush

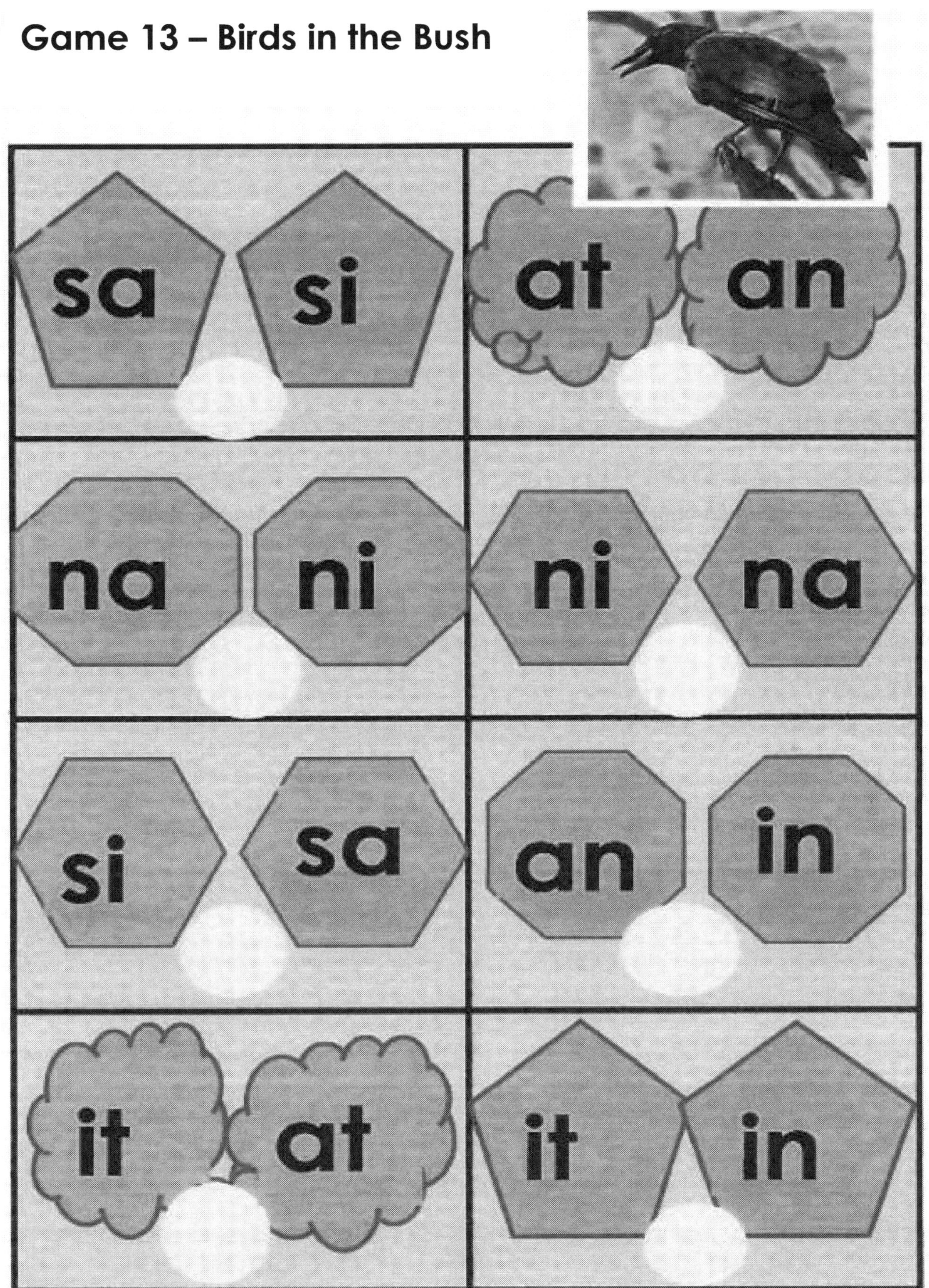

Game 14 – The Detective

You will need letter cards for the letters **a s t n i p**.

Provide a straight horizontal line using masking tape. Stick the tape in a line on the floor, the carpet, or a table.

- Take turns becoming 'The Trickster'. The Trickster selects two letter cards to place *above* the horizontal line (as shown below).
- This player, 'The Trickster', now pronounces the sound of just ***one*** of the two letters.
- The other player, 'The Detective', listens very carefully to the sound pronounced. He selects the letter that 'makes' the sound he heard and places it on the line.
- If the 'Detective' was correct, the two players change roles, and two different letters are selected.

n	p

____

Game 15 – Sound Bites

a n t

- Give your child a selection of *three* letter cards. Help your child arrange the cards above a horizontal line or table edge (as shown above).
- Tell your child, 'I'm going to say a sound, a little sound bite, but if you listen REALLY carefully, you might be able to hear TWO sounds in it!'
- Say, 'Okay! Prick up your ears! Are you ready? Listen for *two* sounds!'
- Pronounce a 2-letter word segment like those in Game 13: *sa, si, at, an, na* . . . But be sure that your child has among his three letters on display, *the two letters that will be needed to* spell the sound bite!
- Say the sound *very slowly* several times, drawing out each sound. Ask, 'Can you find the letter that says the *first* sound you hear?'
- When your child selects the correct letter, praise her and help her to place the letter on the line.
- Pronounce the 2-letter sound again, and ask your child to listen for the *second* sound. Ask, 'Can you find the letter for that second sound?' Help your child place this letter card on the line to the right of the first.
- Point to the two letters together, and ask, 'What does the sound bite say?'
- Reward with a tiny 'bite' of something tasty.

Game 16- Two Treats

- Find the Game 13 page. Place *two* tiny treats under all the pairs of bushes.
- Ask your 'little bird' to choose a pair of bushes to sit in, and tell you what each bush says.
- If he succeeds in reading *both* word parts, shower him with praise, and let him eat both treats.
- If not, the treats are left in place until your child is able to sound out and tell you what each bush 'says'.

Blending Letter-Sounds in Words

For a child, blending just the *first two* sounds in a 3-letter word together to make a *new* sound is a bit of a mind-bending leap. In the word *ant*, for example, blending the sounds /a/ + /n/ results in a NEW sound, the sound /an/. This blending of the first two sounds in a word is often the part children find to be the trickiest bit.

If a child experiences immediate success when blending the first two sounds in a word, blending the rest of the sounds in a word will be relatively easy after that. To ensure success, let your child *join you* in blending the first two sounds of a word together and *copy you* to pronounce the NEW 2-letter sound.

Read the list of blending steps below, and you will be well prepared to help your child succeed like a super star in the games that follow.

SIX STEPS TO BLENDING SUCCESS

1) **WHERE:** Ask, 'Can you point to where you should start sounding out this word?' Your child should point to the letter a in the word *ant*.

2) **LENGTHEN:** To give your child more time, let your child sound out the first letter and lengthen its sound. He should say, '/aaaaa/', stretching out the first sound in the word *ant*. (* Be aware that this lengthening of the first sound in a word is only possible if the letter is a vowel or a continuant.)

3) **YOU SOUND AND BLEND;** then your child joins you. When it comes to blending sounds together, you don't want your child to be baffled even for a second. It's best if you sound and blend the first two letters in a word for your child to listen to. Point underneath the first two letters in the word, slide the 1st sound, /a/, into the 2nd sound, /n/, and say the new sound /an/. Now ask your child to join you to slide the sounds /a/ and /n/ together to say /an/. Repeat several times.

4) **YOU POINT:** You point to a part of the word, and ask '*What does this part say?*' Point underneath the letters *an* in the word *ant*, and ask, 'What does this *first part* say?' Point to the letter *t*, and ask, 'And what does this *last part* say?' In response, your child should say, '/an/' and '/t/'.

5) **YOUR CHILD POINTS:** Ask, 'Can *you point to the part of the word that says* /an/? And to *the part that says /t/*?' Your child points to these parts.

6) **DOES THE WORD SAY____?** Ask what the word says. But if your child does not respond right away, just ask, does it say *ant*?' Your child agrees, and then reads the word *ant* several times.

Game 17 – Bits and Pieces

This game provides ideal practice in the six blending steps.

- Before you start, cover up the pictures on the next page.
- Point to first letter on the top line, and ask, 'What does this letter say?' (/**a**/)
- Ask, 'Can you make the sound again and stretch it?' (/**aaa**/)
- Point underneath the 2 letters in the second segment. *You* sound out each letter, sliding the sounds together to say /an/. **(/aaa/ .../n/ .../an/)**
- Now ask your child to join in. 'Can *you* slide these two sounds together with me?' Together, say – '**/aaa/ ... /n/ ... /an/**'. Repeat several times.
- Point under the letters **an,** and ask, 'So what does *this* part say?' (**/an/**)
- Point under the letter **t,** and ask, 'And what does *this last part* say?' **/t/** Repeat several times.
- Ask your child, 'Can you point to the part that says /an/? .... And the part that says /t/?' Repeat, and praise warmly. Repeat the steps outlined above to help your child blend and read the remaining three words.
- Finally, uncover the pictures. Help your child read all the words again, but this time, ask your child to find their matching pictures as well.

Game 17 – Bits and Pieces

Game 18 – Secret Words

- Give your child the 3 letter cards needed to spell one of the four words above.
- Say, 'I will give you some clues to a secret word. See if you can discover what the word is.'
- Pronounce the word very slowly, drawing out each sound.
- Help your child place the letters in the correct order on a straight line. Praise warmly!

WICKEDLY WILY WORD READING GAMES

Game 19 – Fruity Surprises

On the next page, use a blank sheet of paper to cover the pictures and the final letters in each word.

- Help your child sound out the first two letters on line 1: **/sss/.../i/**.
- *Don't wait for your child to blend the two sounds.* You point under the letters and say, **/sss/...../i/....../si/**, as heard in the word *sip*.
- Have your child join in with you as you once more, slowly sound and blend the first two sounds **/sss/ + /i/ ... /si/**. Repeat many times.
- Once your child can read the 2-letter segment, uncover the last letter in the word and see if he can read the whole word: **/si/ + /p/...... *sip***.
- Now uncover the pictures and see if your child can find the picture that matches the word. At every step, praise your child enthusiastically.
- Now help your child read the other words in the same way.
- Once you have completed the page, cover only the pictures and see if your child can sound out, blend, and read the words.
- Finally, place a small surprise treat (tiny piece of fruit, a sticker, etc.) on each picture. See if your child can read each of the words again, locate its matching picture, and collect the treats as he goes.

Game 19 – Fruity Surprises page

s	i	p
n	i	p
p	a	n
p	a	t
p	i	n
t	a	n

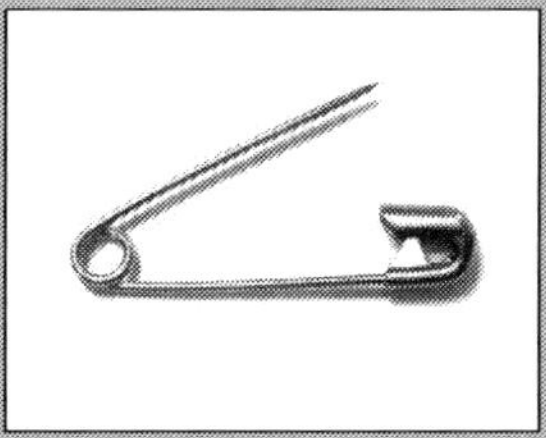

Game 20 – The Blending Accelerator

Point to one of the pictures. Ask if your child can 'make' (spell) the word pictured. Provide the 3 letters. Then see if your child can find the correct word and discover if he/she was right?

Game 21 – The *In a Spin* Reader

This game introduces your child to his first little reading booklet (pp 36- 38).

PAGE 1 (top of p 36):

- Point to the 'cover' and say, 'Now that you can really read, here is your very own book to read!' Point and say, 'This is its *cover*.'
- Now explain, 'People's names always start with a big letter, called a *capital* letter. The names of books do too!' Point to the title, and to each of the words - *In, A, Spin* and explain that the first letter in each word is big, but these letters still say /i/, /a/,and /s/.
- Help your child sound out the 3 words in the title: /i/ + /n/, /a/, /spi/ + /n/. For the word *spin,* make the beginning sound /spi/ for your child to copy.
- Discuss the 3 pictures and help your child sound out the words underneath.

PAGE 1 (bottom):

- Point to the lower half of the page, and say, 'Now let's see what comes next!'
- Follow these four steps:
  1) First, cover up the pictures to increase your child's focus on the print.
  2) Next, help your child sound out each of the words in 2 parts: /si/ + /p/, /pa/+/n/, /pa/ + t/, /ta/+/p/. Praise him warmly after each word.
  3) Now go back, and have him sound out and read the words again. Once he can read the words more quickly, say, 'Wow! That was excellent!'
  4) Next, uncover the pictures. As your child reads each word again, ask, 'Can you find its matching picture?' When your child succeeds, praise excitedly.

PAGE 2 (top of p 37):

- Look at the next page with your child, and follow the same four steps:

  1) Cover up the pictures.
  2) Help your child slowly sound out and read the words in two parts: /ni + /p/, /si/ + /t/, /ti/ + /n/, /i/ +/n/. Praise enthusiastically after each word.
  3) Have your child read the words a second time and congratulate your child: 'Well done! You read that whole page!'
  4) Uncover the pictures, have your child read each word once more, and each time, see if she can find its matching picture. Congratulate.

PAGE 2 (bottom of p 37):

- Follow the same four steps as before: 1) Cover the pictures, 2) Help your child sound out the words once, 3) Help your child sound out and read the words a second time, 4) Uncover the pictures. Help your child read the words again, and find the matching pictures. Praise a lot. You can never praise too much ☺!

PAGE 3 (top of p 37)

- Follow the same four steps.
- On this last page of the reader, the word *pants* appears. Help your child to sound out all the letters to read the word.
- See if she notices the word *tap* on this page has a different meaning than before.

TIME TO SHOW-OFF:

After you and your child have read all the pages in the book together a few times, encourage your child to show off and read her book to others.

In A Spin

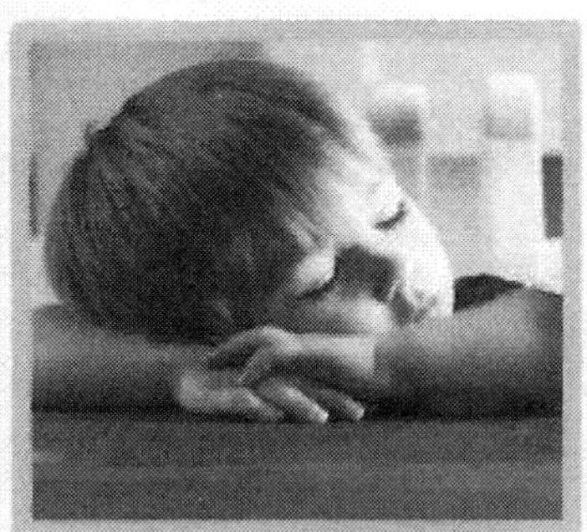

nap

spin

pat

sip pan

pat tap

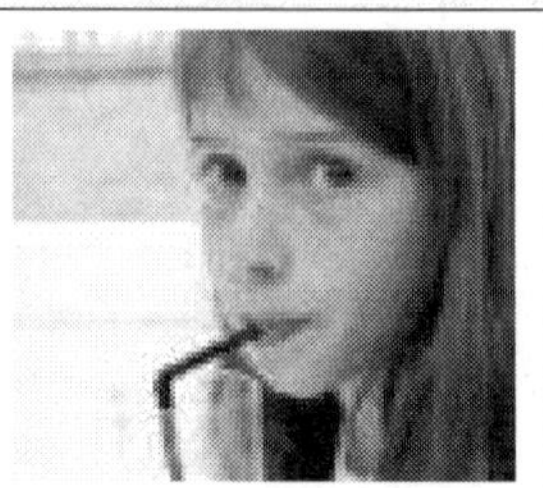

nip sit

tin in

tan tip

pit pips

tap pin

an ant pants

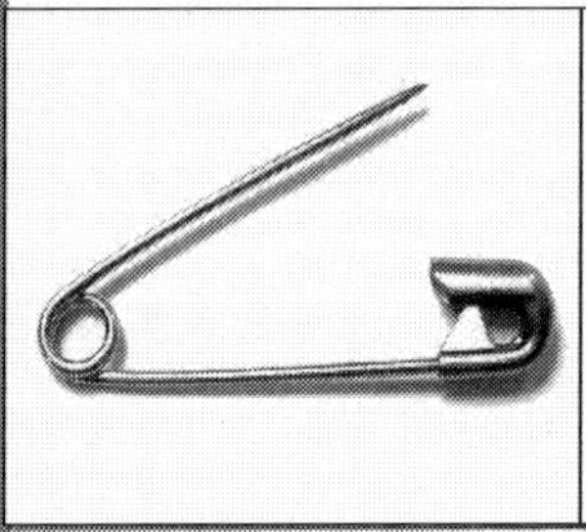

Chapter 2

b o f h u g

Contents

Chapter 2

Welcome to Chapter 2 of *Teach a Child to Read in One Week*. The entertaining games in this chapter will teach your child to:

1) Recognize six more letter shapes: **b, o, f, h, u, g**
2) Remember the sounds they represent: /b/ /o/ /f/ /h/ /u/ /g/
3) Blend new combinations of two letter-sounds together
4) Read two and three letter words, phrases and sentences

So effective are these games, you will be surprised to find that by the end of just one more week, your child will be reading an impressive number of words. Try to play the games every day for at least one session of 20 to 25 minutes. If your child is very young, age 3 or less, you may find that you will need more time to complete the 7-day plan. By the same token, if your child is age 6 or older, you may require less time to complete the games in this chapter. If you miss a day, don't worry. Just refresh your child's memory by replaying some of the games you played previously.

Using the Comic Mnemonics

This book contains another six unique picture and mini-story *Comic Mnemonics*. As in chapter 1, these memory-enhancing devices imprint vital information on your child's long-term memory about: 1) the shapes of letters, and 2) the sounds the letters 'say'.

- Letter-sounds: Remember when you are reading the mini-stories, the letters that appear within slashes - /b/ - indicate the *sound* associated with that letter shape. So pronounce /b/ like the sound heard at the start of the word *bat*, /o/ like the sound you hear at the start of the word *octopus*, and so on.
- The schwa sound: Remember to avoid the schwa sound, keeping your pronunciation for the sound of a consonant as short as possible: /b/, not /buh/, /h/ not /huh/, and /g/ not /guh/.
- Continuants: The letter sound /f/, introduced in this chapter, is a continuant; the sound continues - /fffff/.

- Letter names: Even if your child knows the names of some letters, try to avoid using them. When you are referring to any of the letters in the pictures or mini-stories try to remember to refer to them only by their *sound*.

The time you will need to play the games in this chapter will vary greatly depending on your child's age. With a child as young as 2+ or 3, you are likely to find that short game-playing sessions of no more than 20 minutes will be ideal. Older children are likely to be happy to play for much longer. Feel relaxed about taking the time your child needs to perform well during each game. The main aim is to enjoy yourselves and have fun.

A Suggested 7-Day Plan

DAY

1 Show your child each of the Comic Mnemonic pages for the letters **b o f** (pp 48- 50) . Play Games 1 – 5 with each one.

2 Show your child each of the Comic Mnemonic pages in turn for the letters **h u g** (pp. 51-53). Play Games 1 - 5 with each one. Play Game 6.

3 Play Game 6 again. Then play Games 7, 8 and 9.

4 Play Games 10, 11, and 12.

5 Play Games 13, 14 and the optional game, Game15.

6 Play Game 16, a spelling game. Introduce the *Spit-Spot* reader, Game 17, and spend 15-20 minutes helping your child read it.

7 Continue with Game 17. Encourage your child to read the *Spit-Spot* reader many times, and to read it for friends and family.

Comic Mnemonic Games

Step 1) First, remove a 'Comic Mnemonic Reminder' Card from the Appendix.

Step 2) Next, display one of the Day 1 or 2 Comic Mnemonic pictures (pp 48 – 53).

Step 3) Play all Games 1 - 5 with your child while viewing the mnemonic picture. Detailed instructions for Games 1 – 5 follow. However, when you are both viewing a Comic Mnemonic picture together, you can refer to a 'Comic Mnemonic Reminder' Card to check how to play the five games.

Game 1 – Shifty Shapes

- Read the mini-story to your child. Then read the mini-story a second time while you point out what is happening in the picture.
- Discuss the details of the letter *shape*. Ask, 'What does this letter look like?' Discuss the reasons *why*.
- Ask, 'Can you find another letter in the picture that looks the same?'
- Point to the text and ask, 'Can you find another /b/ (/o/, /f/, /h/, /u/, /g/) here?' (Be sure to say the *sound* of a letter, not its name).
- Point to various individual letter shapes in the picture and the text (not always the target letter), and ask *yes* or *no* questions about the target letter shape: 'Is this a /f/? Is this letter a /g/?' Praise your child's cleverness enthusiastically.

Game 2 – A Sound Story

- Read the story to your child again and ask questions that focus on the letter's *sound*:
- 'What *sound* does the bat hitting the ball/ the octopus/ the flower/ the high chair/ the baby with arms up/ the girl make? What sound does it make again?'
- Ask WHY the letter makes a certain sound. (The bat is hitting the ball, the octopus is worried about the hot water, the flower flutters in the wind, the high chair has a cushion that huffs, the baby wants to be picked *up*, and the girl is giggling.
- Ask your child to make the letter sound in different voices. For /b/, loud and aggressive, for /o/, alarmed and frightened, for /f/, soft and gentle, for /h/, breathless, for /u/, tiny, baby, for /g/, happy and giggling.
- The aim is to have your child *say the sound* of the letter as many times as possible in response to looking at the letter's shape. Praise your child's efforts heartily.

Game 3 – Talking Letters

- Read the story again. Focus on having your *child say the sound* of a letter while you point to it and describe its shape.
- Point to details in the *illustration* and ask, 'What does this bat and ball shaped letter say? What does it say again?'
- Point to the letters that appear in the *text*, and ask, 'What does this letter say? And, this one? And what about this letter?' Repeat many times.
- Point to letters other than the target letter to check that your child is not on 'automatic pilot'.
- Find examples of particular letter shapes on packaging or tins while you are out shopping, and ask, 'Do you remember what this letter *says*?'
- Praise your child lavishly.

Game 4 - Let's Clown Around

- Read the story again but this time, you and your child can adopt the letter shapes, and act out the letter's character. Together, be as silly as you can be.
- Depending on the story, pretend to be:

  Either the bat or ball, one bumping the other (gently) saying '/b/,/b/,/b/'

  An octopus with waving arms and legs, shouting, '/o/,/o/,/o/!'

  A flower, neck bent, swaying in the wind, softly saying '/fff/, /fff/, /fff/'

  A chair with knees bent, huffing. '/h/, /h/, /h/'

  A little baby on the floor, arms held straight up, crying out, '/u/, /u/, /u/!'

  A girl, with something on her head to resemble a pony tail, giggling, '/g/, /g/, /g/.'

Game 5 – Song and Dance Routine

- Give your child one of the chapter 2 letters. Remove page 55 and cut out the lower case letter cards as needed,
- Have your child compare the letter to the one in a Comic Mnemonic picture, and ask, 'Does this letter look the *same* as the one in this picture?'
- Ask, 'Can you put it the right way up, beside one that looks exactly the same?'
- Once your child does this correctly, it becomes the signal to begin the *Song and Dance* routine. Encourage your child to chant the mini-story to a tune you make up while your child makes the letter dance around.

/b/ looks like

A big, bad bat – so tall

Right beside a roly-poly ball

Bat gives the bumbling ball such thumps

Can you hear the /b/ /b/ /b/ bumps?

Octopus sees

A very big pot

'/o/ - /o/ - /o/!'

He hollers

'That's way too hot!'

/f/ looks like a flower having fun

A gentle wind fans it in the sun

'/ f f f /' - listen as it flits and flutters

Can you hear the soft sound it mutters?

'/ f f f f f /'

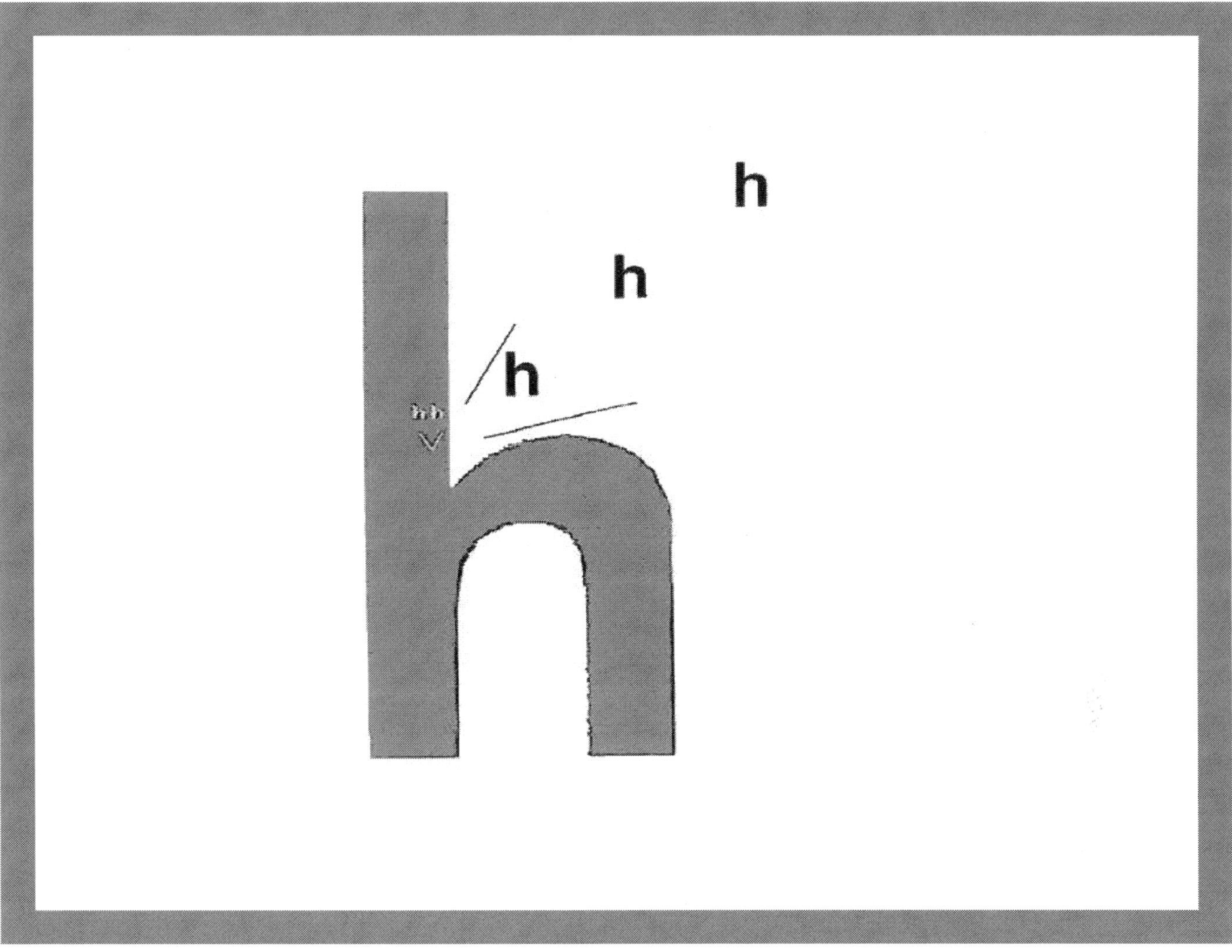

/h/ looks like

A huffy, puffy, high chair

With a humpy seat

'/h/ /h/ /h/' he huffs

When you sit on him to eat

/u/ is holding both hands up

Just like a baby

Who wants to come

'/u/ - /u/ - /u/' – up!

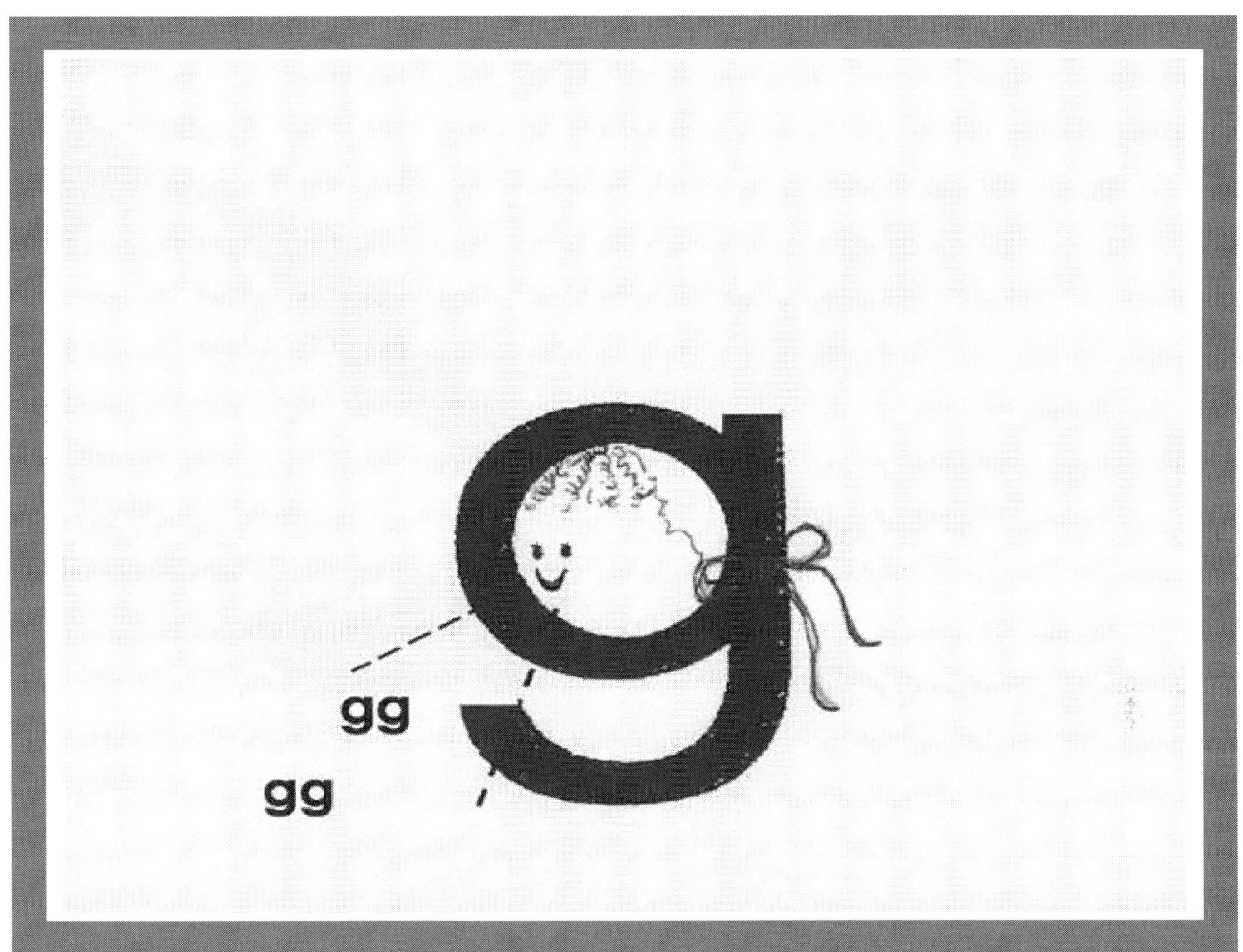

/g/ like a girl all a-jiggle

Her hair goes down in a squiggle

If you listen – '/g/ /g/ -/g/ /g/'

You can hear her girlish giggle

Game 6 – Seek and Speak

To review, look back over all the Comic Mnemonic pictures on pages 48 to 53.

- Ask, 'Can you find a picture where the letter looks like a high chair, a giggling girl, a fluttering flower, a baby with its arms up, an octopus, a bat and ball?
- Point to various letters and ask, 'What does this letter say?'
- Point to letters and ask *why* questions about the sound a letter makes: 'Why does this letter say /b/ (/o/, /f/, /h/, /u/, /g/)?' PRAISE highly.
- Now show your child the smaller pictures in the box above, and play the game again.

Lower case letter cards

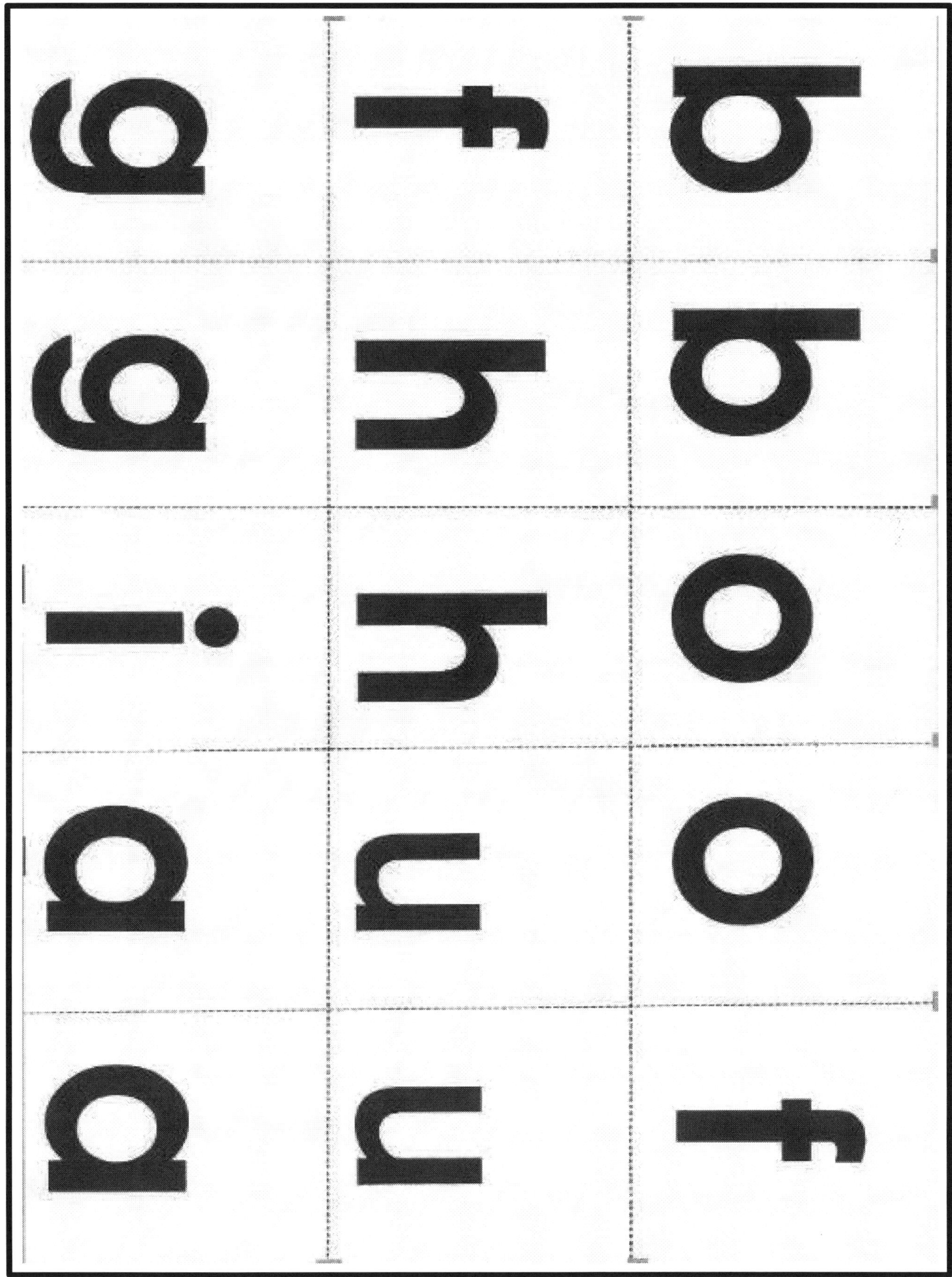

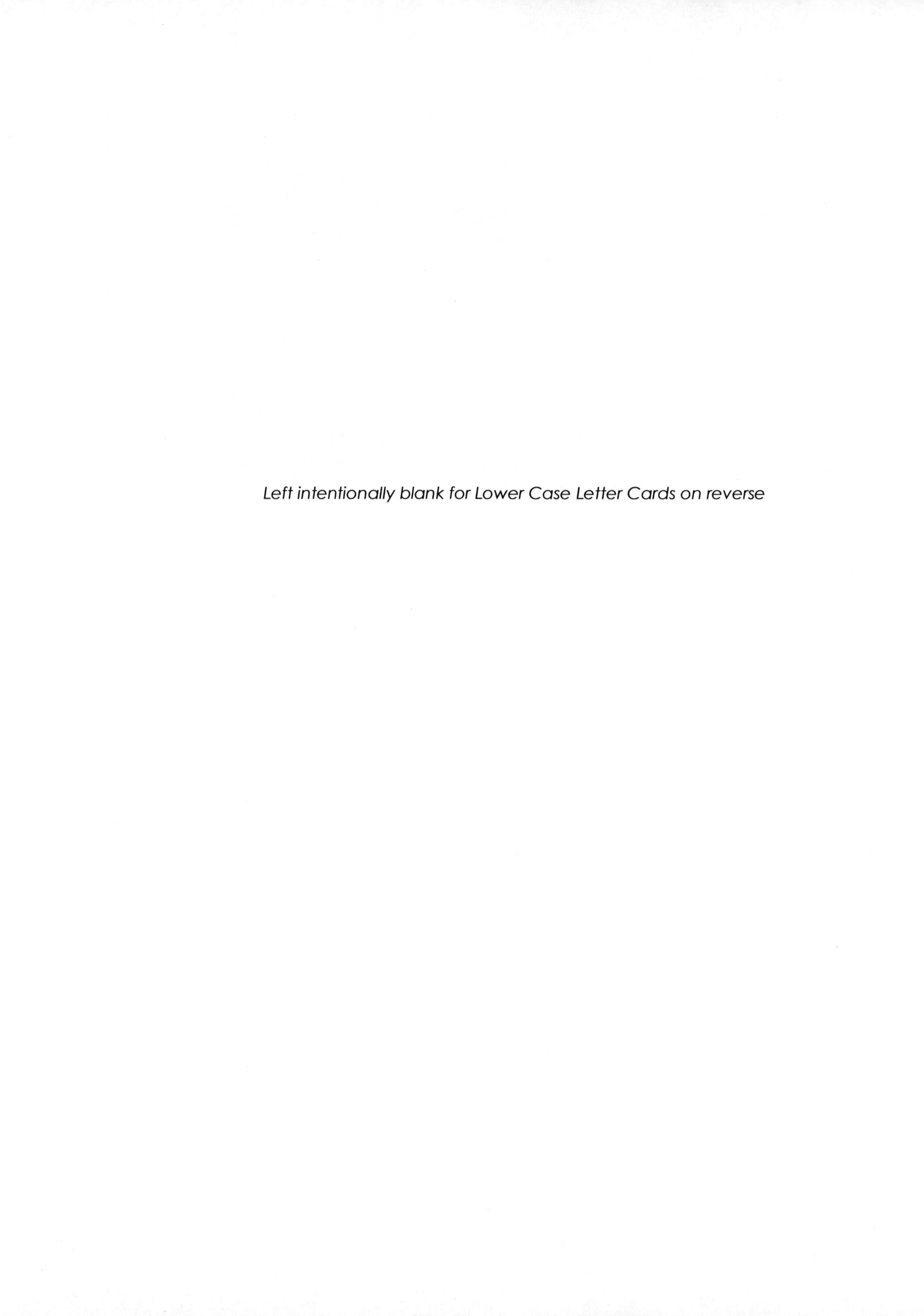

Left intentionally blank for Lower Case Letter Cards on reverse

Game 7 – Giant Seek and Speak

If you are confident your child knows the six Chapter 2 letter shapes and sounds, tell him that he might be clever enough for this next game. Display the following page which shows all 12 of the Chapter 1 and 2 Comic Mnemonic pictures.

- Ask, 'Can you find a letter that *looks like* . . . ?'
- Ask, 'Can you find the letter that *says* . . . ?'
- Point to letters and ask what sound they make.
- Keep playing until your child can perform without hesitating.
- Reward with lots of enthusiastic praise and hugs throughout.
- Then let your child test *you*. But, be sure to make some silly mistakes from time to time to encourage your child to remain on the alert.

Game 7 – Giant Seek and Speak

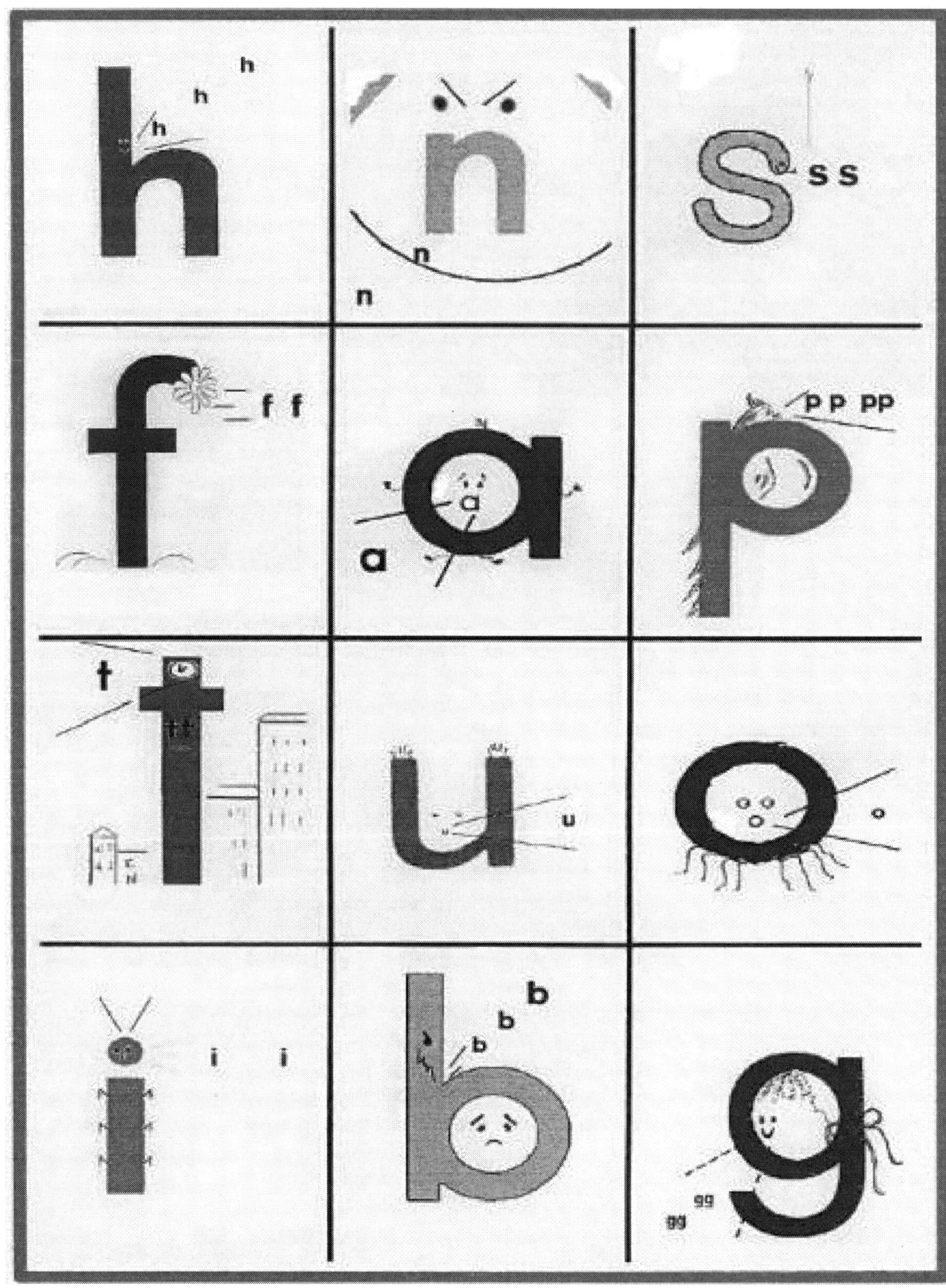

LICKETY SPLIT LETTER-SOUND GAMES

Game 8 – Up to Double Trouble

- Select letters your child knows so far. Place the letters **u** and **p** at the bottom of some stairs and one letter on each of the steps. Place a reward at the top.
- *To start*: The first player pushes the two letters together to make the word *up*.
- Players then take turns making the letter on each step 'talk'.
- Whichever player reaches the top step first, collects the reward.
- Play often with different letters. Always begin the game by spelling *up*.
- *For a double reward*: a player must make a full staircase of letters 'talk'.

☝ Game 9 – Sneaky Snakes Hide and Squeak

- Turn the next page sideways so your child can see the snake faces. Or, see the ***Introduction, page xiii*** for an explanation of this hand symbol - ☝.
- Use a piece of paper to cover up everything except the snake faces.
- Ask your child to choose one Sneaky Snake to 'play' with.
- Then, one by one, uncover the letters hiding on the snake.
- Explain that these snakes like to hide, so each time they are uncovered they are inclined to squeak!
- Ask your child each time, 'Can you make this letter 'squeak?'
- If your child is correct, praise warmly and uncover the next letter.
- Encourage your child to 'squeak' all the way to the tail end.
- When fluent with one snake, let your child choose another. PRAISE warmly.
- When your child can complete all four snakes, reward with a special treat!

Game 9 – Sneaky Snakes Hide and Squeak

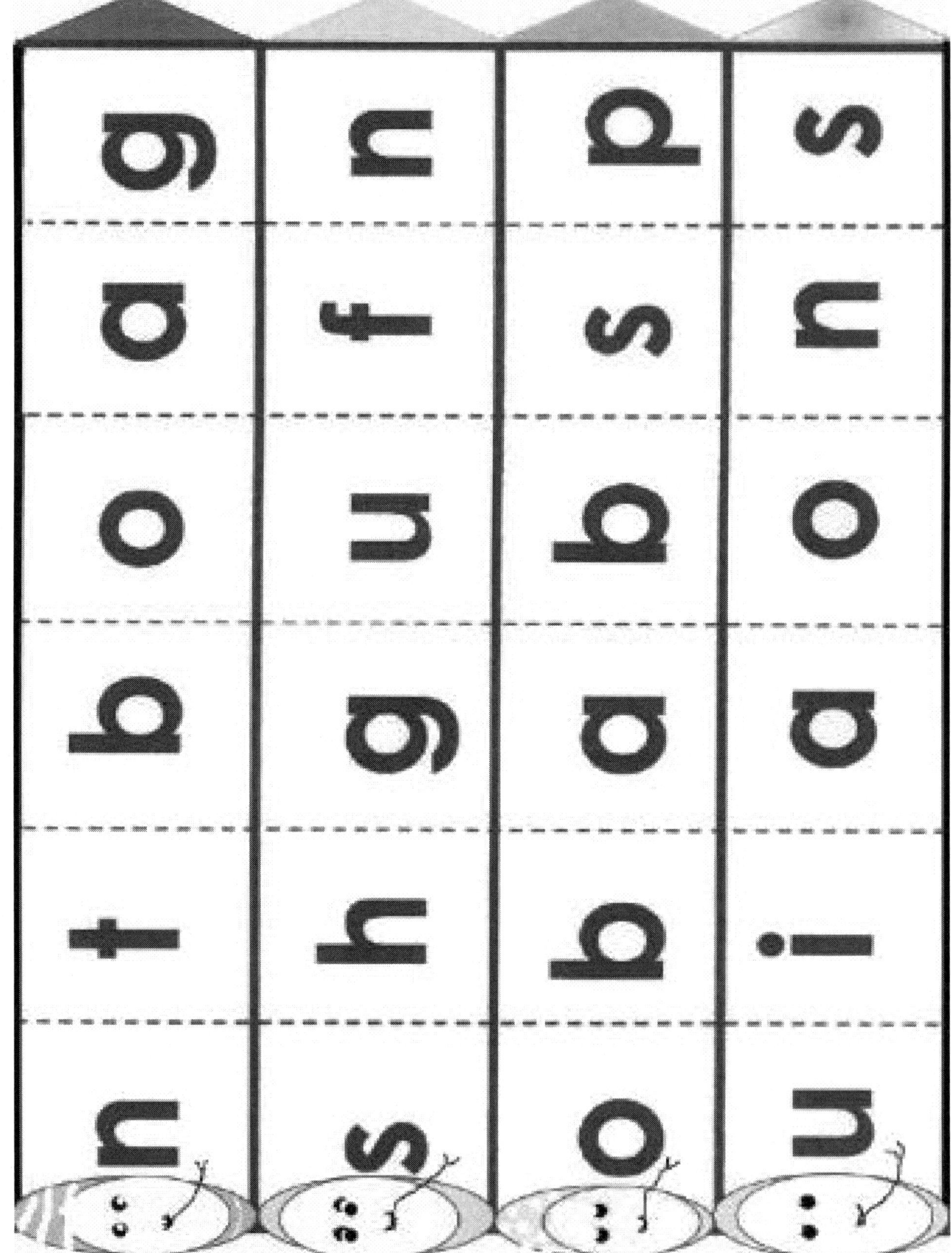

MIND-BENDING SOUND BLENDING GAMES

Remember just blending two letter-sounds together can be a mind-bending challenge for young readers! These four steps can make it easier:

1) Ask your child to point to *where he should start* sounding out.

2) If the first sound is a vowel or a continuant, have him *lengthen* the sound before saying the second sound. (This lengthening doesn't work for **p**, **b**, and **g**.)

3) Don't hesitate to say the new 2-letter sound *for your child to copy.*

4) Pointing one by one underneath to each of the two letters, have your child slowly sound out and then *say the new 2-letter sound*, repeating it several times.

Game 10 – Snippets

- Number five pieces of paper from one to five. Put them in a container.
- Let your child choose one and find the number chosen on the next page.
- Explain, 'This creature' (point to it) 'needs help finding his favourite snack.'
- Ask, 'Can you help the bee (/ frog/ hummingbird/ rabbit/ seagull) say the sound of each of these word parts so he can find his favourite snack?'
- Remember, to begin with anyway, YOU may need to say each 2-letter segment *for your child to copy*. To pronounce the segments correctly just think of a word that begins with those 2 letters. Continue to help with this until your child can pronounce the entire trail of sound segments fluently on his own.
- When your child is fluent with a trail of sounds, reward with a tiny snack.

Game 10 – Snippets

Game 11 – Sharp Eyes

Turn the next page sideways, and show your child the 3 word columns.

Cover two of them with a sheet of paper. Explain, 'You need to have very sharp eyes to play this game. Tell me when you are ready!'

1) First sound in a word:

- Pointing to the word column now on display, and say, 'Every one of these words has something that is the *same* about them? Can you see what it is?'
- See if your child notices that all the words start with the *same letter-sound.* if not, point to the first letter in each word and ask, 'What does this say?'
- Praise and follow the same procedure with the other two word columns.

2) Initial, two-letter, blended sounds in words:

- Next, ask your child to choose *one* of the three word columns. Cover the final letters in all the words so that only the first two letters of each word are seen.
- Ask, in random order, '*Can you find* the word part that says /ni/, /no/, /nu/... /si/, /su/, /sa/... /fa/, /fi/, /fu/?'* To pronounce the sounds correctly, it helps to think of a word starting with those two letters.
- Ask your child to *point underneath* the initial two letters of each word, and ask, 'What does that two-letter part say again?'
- Play the game again with the remaining two word columns.
- Shower your sharp-eyed child with praise throughout.

*Note that sometimes, *more than one word* starts with the target word part. So always ask, 'Is there another word that starts with that *same* sound?'

Game 11 – Sharp Eyes word columns

nib	not	nut	nag
sit	sat	sun	sag
fin	fan	fun	fat

Game 12 – Fan Fun

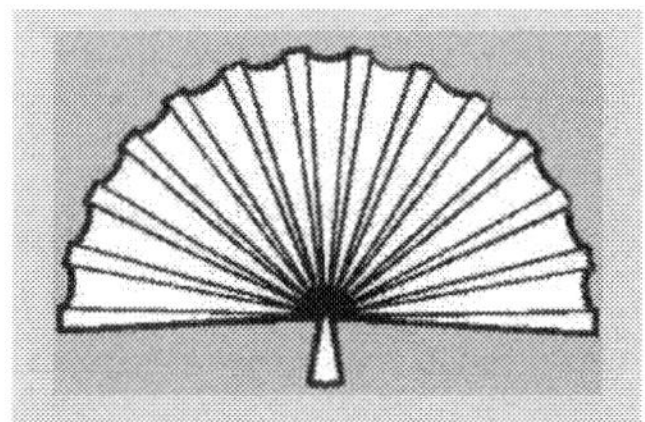

- Ask your child to choose one of the word columns on the previous page.
- Point to the *first two letters* in each word, asking, 'What does *this* part say? *Don't let your child struggle*; remember to provide the sound for her to copy if necessary. Praise highly.
- Once you have done this for every word in the column, return your child's attention to the top of the list.
- Point underneath to the first two letters of the word, and ask, 'What does *this part* say again?' Then, point underneath to the last letter of the word, and ask, 'And what does *this last part* say?'
- Have her repeat the sounds of the first, and last parts of the word, and see if she can read the word. Give help as needed until your child can read all four words in the column without help. Repeat the whole operation for the other 2 columns.

Game 13 – One, Two, Three, Magic!

- Show your child the next page and ask, 'Do you want to make magic?'
- Give him a 'magic wand' (a ruler/ wooden spoon). Say, 'Just take the three, sound-blending steps then wave your magic wand and say the secret word!'
- Help your child sound out the word parts, waving his 'wand' after step 3.

Game 13 – One, Two, Three, Magic!

1	2	3
h	ha	ha t
f	fi	fi g
p	po	po p
h	ho	ho p
p	pi	pi g
t	to	to p
b	ba	ba t
f	fa	fa t
b	bi	bi g

WICKEDLY WILY WORD READING GAMES

Game 14 – Let's Go and Ski!

- Point out to your child how the next page looks like a big snowy mountain.
- Point to the chair lift on the left side. Pretend to get on the lift at the bottom and zoom up to the top of the mountain.
- At the top, say, 'Let's see if we can ski down the mountain!' Follow the ski tracks.
- Help your child sound out the words one by one: ha +t, to +p, nu +t...
- Praise, and encourage your child to 'ski' to the bottom for a treat in the lodge.
- Then zoom back up the mountain on the chair lift, invite your child to ski down again, read the words, and collect another treat.

Game 15 – Hunting Lost Hats ☝

- Play this game to give your child more word reading practice.
- Tell your child to close her eyes and point to the mountain.
- Ask your child to keep her finger on the page, open her eyes, and see 'What is the nearest word?
- Help your child sound out the word, and do her best to remember it.
- Say, 'It's important to remember it because this is *the lost item* to be found.'
- Now take the chair lift, to top of the mountain together. Pretend to ski down and help your child read the words along the way.
- Your child then tries to read this word without your help.
- If correct, she can now ski to the bottom of the mountain, without stopping to read any of the rest of the words.
- Congratulate, and let her collect a treat at the lodge.
- Repeat the game as many times as you like.

hat
top
nut
bat
pop
fan
bun
pig
bug
hut

Game 16 – The *Spit-Spot* Reader

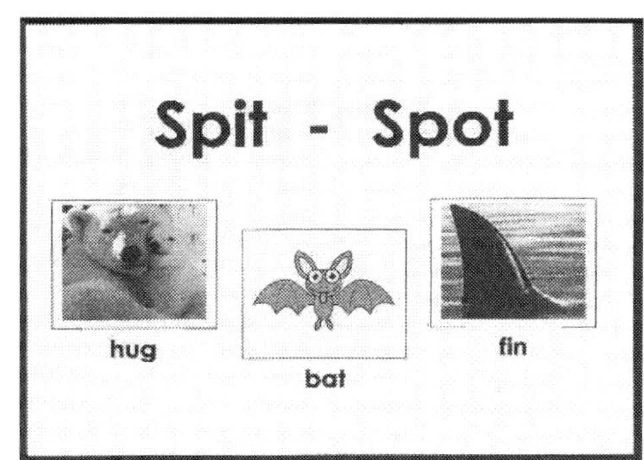

This game introduces your child to his second reading booklet.

PAGE 1 (top):

- Cover the lower half of the page. Tell your child, 'Now that you can read so well, here is another little book especially for you.
- Show your child the book's cover page and ask, 'Can you read the name of it?' Have your child point underneath to every letter in the two words, as together, you very slowly sound out and read: ***S p i t – S p o t***. (You can help your child by making the beginning sounds of each word - /spi/ and /spo/ - for your child to copy.
- Discuss the pictures and help your child read the words underneath.

PAGE 1 (bottom)

- Then say, 'Let's see what comes next!' Uncover the lower half of the page, and follow these four steps:
    1) Cover up the pictures to increase your child's focus on the print.
    2) Help your child sound out each of the words in 2 parts: /fi/+/n/, /ta/+/g/, /hu/+/g/, /ga/+/s/. Praise warmly after each word.
    3) Now go back, and help your child read the words again until he can read all the words quickly. Be sure to tell your child how clever he is.
    4) Next, uncover the pictures, and as your child reads each word again, ask, 'Can you *spot* the matching picture?' PRAISE excitedly.

PAGES 2 – 5:

- Use a blank sheet of paper to cover the lower half of each new page.
- Then for each half page, follow the same four steps outlined on the previous page.

While reading the booklet together, point out the following to your child:

1) Double consonants: On the final pages of the reader, the name *Ann* and the words *huff* and *puff* appear. Simply explain to your child that whenever he sees two letters the same together (**nn** and **ff**), they make just one sound, (/n/, /f/).

2) Capital letters: Explain that *Bob, Gus, Ann* and *Pat* are people's names. Explain that a person's name always starts with a big, important letter (called a 'capital' letter) because *people are important*. If your child can print his name, he may be acquainted with this convention.

3) Irregularly spelled words or *Tricky Words*: On the last page, two underlined, irregularly spelled words appear. If your child sounds out the word ***is*** as /iss/, (and the word ***has*** as /hass/), say, 'That is a good try! But wait a minute!' Ask, 'Is there actually a word like that?' Together, decide *there is no such word*. Explain that, 'The words underlined here are 'Tricky Words'. These are words that do not follow the rules. Instead, they want to trick you!'

4) Back cover lists the Tricky Words Point to the tricky-looking cat on the lower half of the page (the back cover of the book). Explain, 'On the back cover of the book, all the Tricky Words in this book are listed. Can you find that Tricky Word listed here?' Congratulate your child for finding it. Then remind your child that there is no such word as /iss/ (or, /hass/). Ask your child to guess what the word might *really* say. Praise, 'Well done! That word tried to trick you. But it didn't trick YOU, did it?' Point to how the word should have been spelled /iz/ (/haz/).

TIME TO SHOW-OFF:

Encourage your child to entertain friends and family by reading his booklet to them.

Spit - Spot

hug

bat

fin

fin

tag

hug

gas

a pup

a bag

a pot

a hat

nuts

in a tub

figs

on a bus

a big pig

a big pup

fat Bob

big Gus

in a sub

in fog

a hot bun

a big tug

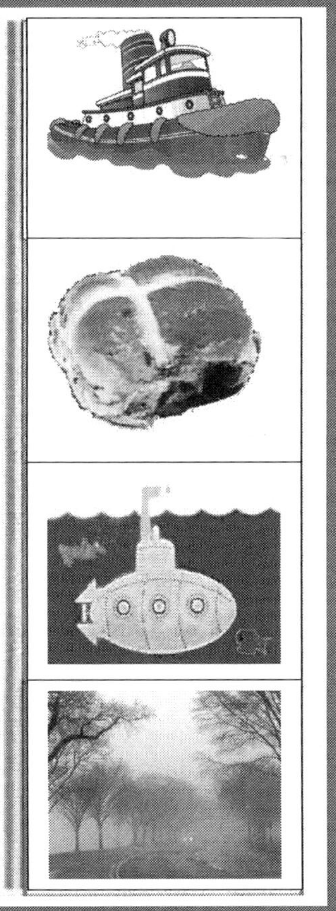

Ann hops.

Stop at it.

It fits in.

Bob pops it.

on a hunt

huff n' puff

spots on a bug

a bib on Pat

It <u>is</u> not fast.

It <u>has</u> spots.

A pig <u>has</u> fun.

It has fins.

Tricky words in this book

is	**has**
(iz)	(haz)

Chapter 3

l e m d r c (k ck)

Contents

cap
cat
red

Chapter 3

Congratulations on your efforts so far. By now, your child has developed important insights into what reading is all about. He knows that:

- words have a number of letters in them,
- the letters can be translated into sounds, and
- if he blends the sounds together he will discover what the word 'says'.
- He will, in fact, be able to *read* the word!

Even if you stop playing these reading games right now, you have given your child a certain amount of valuable insurance against reading failure. In effect, what you have given your child is a secret weapon. Your child now knows that reading is not as mysterious as he might have thought. He doesn't have to guess, or memorize. He has a strategy that works.

The need for protection

However, your child seriously *does* need a secret weapon. In many classrooms today, children are given the idea that the process of reading involves remembering whole words. They are taught that words should be memorized based on: the word shape, the sentence context, or the pictures that accompany them. Believe it or not, right at the very start of beginning reading instruction, children are exposed to this 'reading' approach. This approach, however, requires memorizing words, not reading them.

So even though the *Teach a Child to Read in One Week* games you have played so far have given your child a promising head start, he may not yet be ready to withstand a heavy dose of whole word memorization and guessing instruction. Many clever young children have good memories and can adopt this approach all too easily.

Instead of sounding out words and developing the neural networks in the brain *required* for real reading, countless children are being detoured down a slow and dangerous road. It is *slow* because children are forced to deduce letter-to-sound relationships for themselves, or if this knowledge is taught directly at all, it may take several years in school before all the facts are covered. It is *dangerous* because children soon find themselves in a situation where, without pictures, previously memorized sentences, and a familiar story, they have no means whatsoever of unlocking the words on a page.

How Irregular Is the English Language?

Teachers often justify teaching children to memorize whole words based on their belief that the English language has too many difficult-to-sound-out, irregularly spelled words. And the truth? *More than two-thirds of the most frequently used words in English have spellings that are regular, follow rules, and are easy to sound out*. The deliberate delay and gradual introduction of irregularly spelled words in these games is designed to encourage your child to feel confident about the sounding out strategy he is using.

Chapter 3 Introduces:

- Six new sounds: / l / / e/ / m/ / d/ / r/ / c/, and
- Eight new spellings for those sounds: **l e m d r c k ck**

Here's how to pronounce the sounds-

- /l/, like the first sound heard in the word *lick*; /l/, not /luh/
- /e/, like the first sound heard in the word *egg,*
- /m/, like the first sound heard in the word *muffin*: /m/ not /muh/, and the sound continues - /mmmm/
- /d/, as heard at the start of the word *drink*: /d/ not /duh/
- /r/, as heard at the start of the word *rocket*: /r/ not /ruh/; the sound continues so it's easier to think of the sound as a long, continuing /er/ sound
- /c/ and /k/ as heard in the word *cough* or *kid*: /c/ not /cuh/
- /ck/ as heard in the words *cough*, *kid* or *sock*: /c/ not /cuh/

Using the Comic Mnemonics

Eight new mnemonic pictures and mini-stories are included in this chapter. Two new letters are introduced at a time, and the games which follow practise letter-to-sound translation, sound blending, and word reading. Try to play the games for about 20 minutes a day. Above all, have fun!

A Suggested 7-Day Plan

Day

1 Play Games 1, 2, 3, and 4, which include Comic Mnemonic, Letter-Sound translation, Sound Blending and Word Reading games that introduce the new letters **l** and **e**.

2 Play Games 5, 6, and 7, which introduce the new letters **m** and **d**.

3 Play Games 8, 9 and 10, which introduce the new letters **r** and **c**.

4 Play Games 11, 12, and 13.

5 Play Games 14, 15, 16, and 17.

6 Play Games 18, 19, and 20.

7 Play Game 21, the *Flip-Flap* reader, which may require two game-playing sessions.

Comic Mnemonic Games

Game 1 – The Long and Short of It

☺ Comic Mnemonic Games

Point to page 85. Focus on one picture at a time, covering up the other one.

For the letter 'l':

- Read the mini-story, and ask, 'What is sticking out of the boy's mouth? (his tongue) 'Why does the boy have his tongue sticking out?' (he's licking) 'What is it he is licking?'(ice-cream) 'What shape is the boy's tongue?' (long and thin with a curl on the lower end)
- Read the story again. Point to any letter '**l**' in the picture or the story and ask, 'What *sound* does this letter make? And, this one?' (/l/ - like the sound you hear at the beginning of the word *lick*)
- Ask, '*Why* does the boy's tongue say /l/? (it's making a licking sound)

For the letter 'e':

- Read the mini-story and ask, 'What is this underneath the /e/?'(an egg cup) Ask, 'What does the /e/ look like?' (an egg)
- Read the story once more. Ask, 'What *sound* does the /e/ make?' (/e/) Point to any letter 'e' in the picture or the story and ask, 'What sound does this letter make?' (/e/)
- Ask, '*Why* does this letter say/e/?' (he's upset that there's a crack in his side and he's leaking)
- Ask, '*Why* does this letter say/e/?' (he's upset that there's a crack in his side and he's leaking)

Game 1 – The Long and Short of It

/l/ is long and
lean
like a
stick!
Like a
tongue
that
goes
lick, lick,
lick!

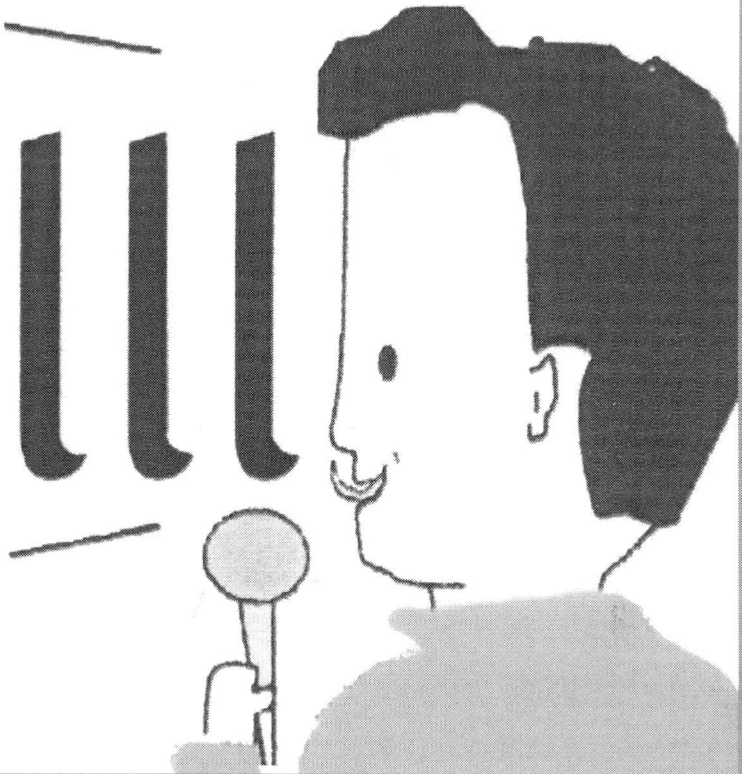

/e/, /e/,
/e/ is like an egg
round and fat like a
keg. '/e/, /e/, /e/', he says
'I seem to have a leak!
A crack in my side!
Oh! /e/, /e/, /e/
- eek!'

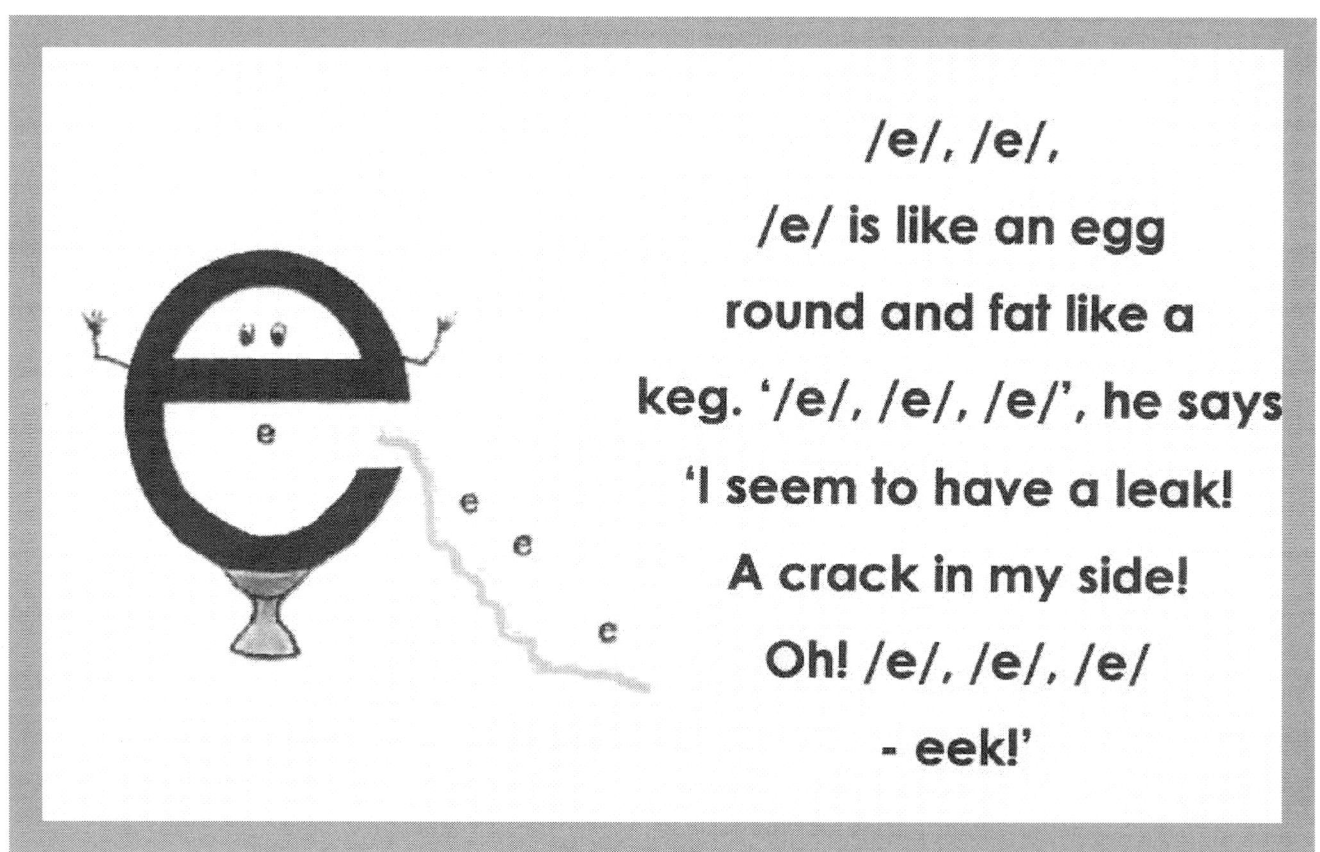

Game 2 - Letter Fun

A Lickety-Split Letter-Sound Game

- Show your child the box below.
- Point to different letters, asking what *sound* each one makes.
- Ask your child if she can *find a letter* in response to your saying its sound:

  'Can you find a letter that says . . . ?'

- Provide plenty of enthusiastic praise throughout.

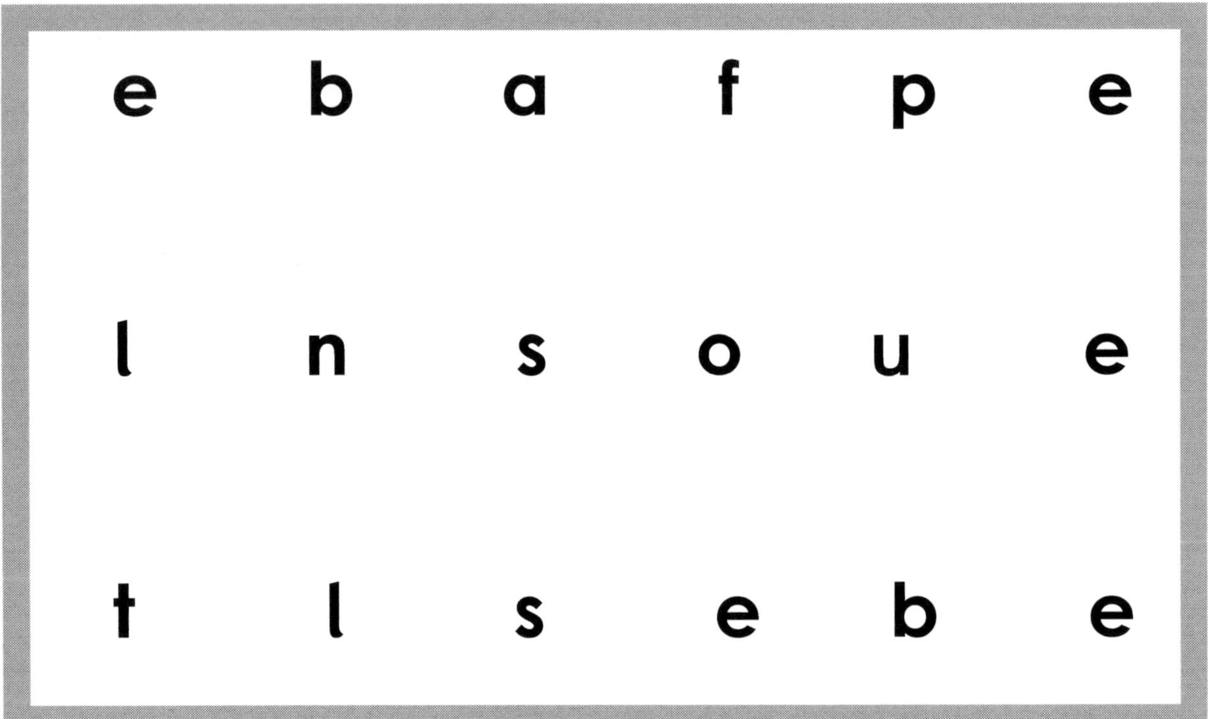

Game 3 - Ella the Forgetful Hen

❖ *A Mind-Bending Sound Blending Game*

- Explain that Ella, the hen below, can't remember where she left her egg.
- Ask, 'Can follow the crumbs, say the sounds as you go, and help Ella find her egg?'
- At first, you can pronounce the sound for your child to copy. Give lots of praise. (These 2-letter sounds are pronounced like the sounds you can hear at the start of the words: ***be**d*, ***ge**t*, ***le**t*, ***la**p*, ***fe**ll*, ***lo**g*, ***se**ll*, ***lu**ck*, ***te**ll*, ***li**ck*, ***se**t*, ***pe**n*.)

Game 4 – Hen Hunt ✋

📖 *A Wickedly Wily Word Reading Game*

- Explain that the words on the next page are the names of hens.
- Some of the hens have very peculiar names!
- Take turns selecting a 'hen' and reading its 'name'. If necessary, help your child read the word in two parts -/ lo/ + /g/
- If correct, the player can keep that hen, and give it a treat. 'Hen treats' might be small egg-shaped items (a peanut, raisin, jelly bean, etc.)
- The hen treat should be left in place on top of the word that was read.
- Tell your child that the words: *e**gg***, *gu**ll***, and *be**ll***, found in this game, follow the same rule as the words *Ann*, *huff* and *puff* in Chapter 2: 'When the *same* two letters are together, they make just *one* sound.')
- When it is your turn to select a hen and read its name, make occasional mistakes to check that your child is monitoring you carefully.
- When all the hens' names have been read, players take turns *collecting* the treats by finding their hens, and reading their names once more.

Game 4 – Hen Names

l	o	g	l	e	g
l	a	p	l	i	p
h	e	n	t	e	n
e	g	g	p	e	n
g	u	ll	b	e	ll

Game 5 – Muffins, Donuts and Drinks

☺ Comic Mnemonic Games

Point to page 91, and to ensure your child concentrates on one picture at a time, cover up the other one.

For the letter 'm' picture:

- Read the mini-story and ask questions such as: 'What is this part below the muffin?' (the paper muffin cup) 'What do you think the little round bits on the muffin might be?'(blueberries, raisins . .)'Why are there wiggly lines arising from the top of the muffin?' (steam rising)'How many mounds does this muffin have?' (two)
- Read the story once more, point to the target letter **m** (in the story or picture) and ask, 'What does this letter *say*?' (/mmm/, not /muh/.)
- Ask, '*Why* does the muffin say, /mmmmm/?' (he thinks he is so yummy)

For the letter 'd' picture:

- Point and ask, 'What does this round part of the /d/ look like?'(a donut) 'What does this long tall part of /d/ look like?' (a drink) Why is this round part of the letter right next to the tall drink part? (the donut, which is probably very sticky, is *stuck* to the drink) 'What is this object in the drink?' (a straw)
- Read the story once more, point to the target letter **d** (in either the picture or the story) and ask, 'What does this letter say? And this one?' (Try to keep the sound short - /d/, not /duh/))
- Ask, '*Why* does this letter make a dumb /d/ sound?' (he doesn't know how to think)

As a review:

- Keep both pictures on view. Ask your child to point to the picture where the letter *looks like*: a donut *stuck to* a drink or, a muffin.
- Ask your child to find and point to any letter in either picture that *says*: /m/ or /d/).

Game 5 – Muffins, Donuts, and Drinks

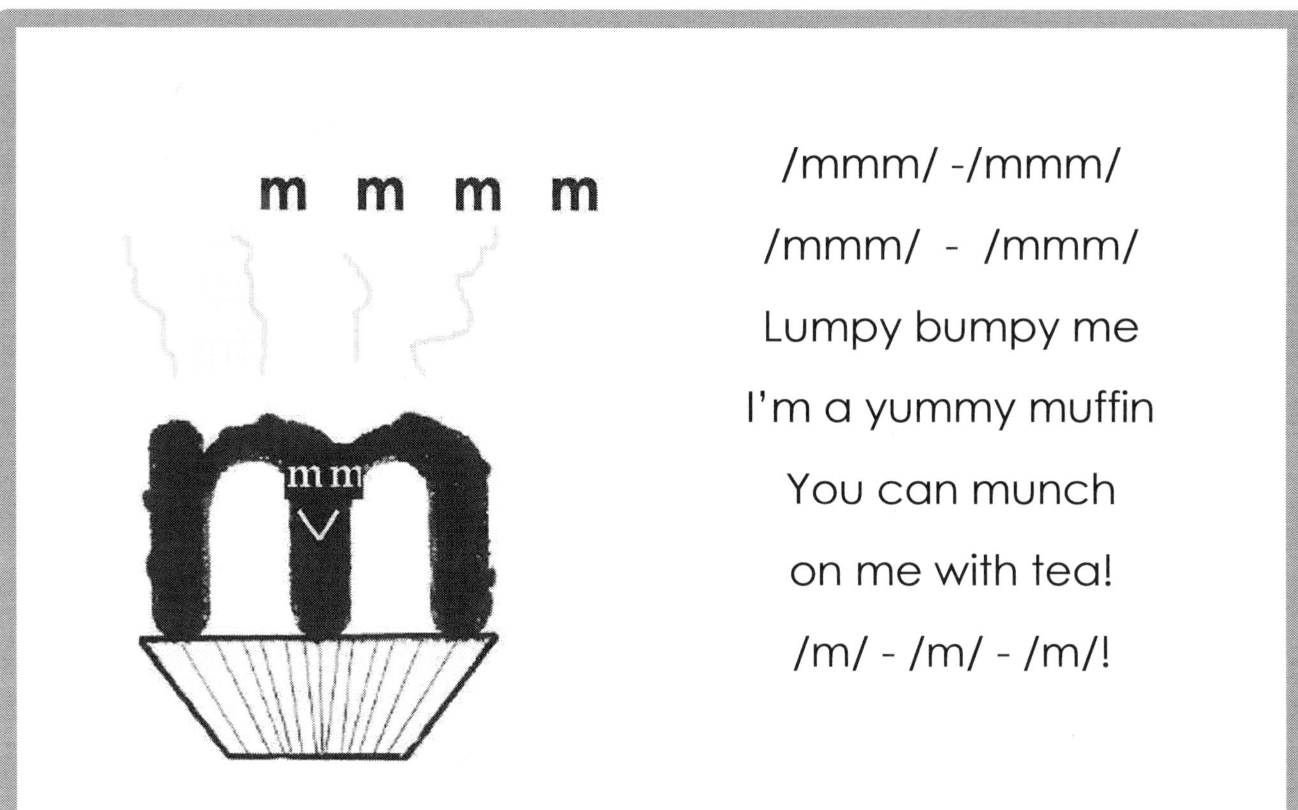

/d/looks like a donut
Sitting down by a drink
'/d/ . . /d/ . . /d/ . .'
Is the dumb,
dumb
dizzle
he doozles
Since he doesn't
know how to think!

Game 6 – Letter Mess

❢ *A Lickety-Split Letter-Sound Game*

- Point to the box below. Ask, 'Can you find any letters that say /d/, /e/, /m/ or /l/?'
- Now ask your child to give the sound of all the letters, moving from the left to the right for each row of letters.
- Ask your child to find all letters that look like: a long licking tongue, an egg with a leak, a lumpy, bumpy muffin, a donut stuck to a drink.
- Ask your child to find all letters that look like: a long licking tongue, an egg with a leak, a lumpy, bumpy muffin, a donut stuck to a drink.
- Let your child point to letters for *you* to say their sounds. (Don't always give the correct sound, a ploy that will increase your child's attention.)

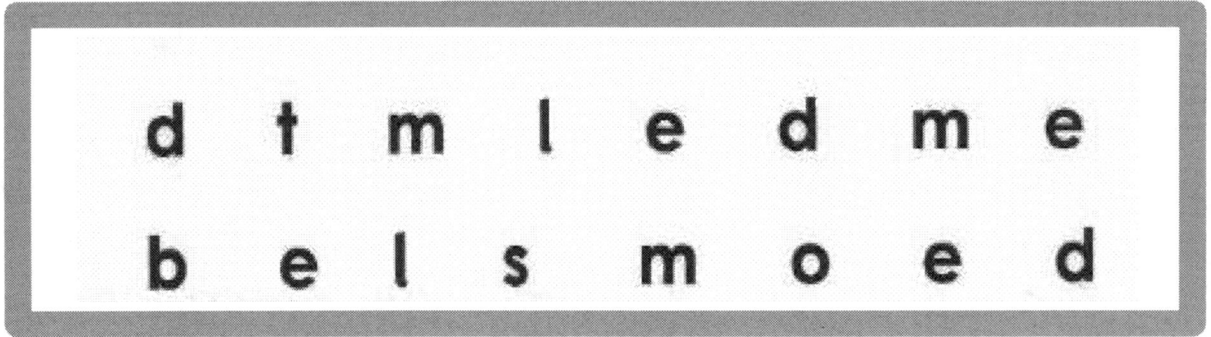

Game 7 – Hide and Seek

❖ *A Mind-Bending Sound Blending Game*

- Show your child the next page, and *hide the last letters of all the words*.
- For each word, help your child sound out the beginning 2-letter segment. If necessary, pronounce the sound for him to copy and repeat it.
- Then show him the last letter and see if he can read the whole word. Praise highly.

Game 7 - Hide and Seek words

mug	dog
mill	mess
dam	mud
dig	map
bed	dots

Game 8 – Hunt High and Low

A Wickedly Wily Word Reading Game

Take turns reading the words that follow. *Both* players then hunt high and low to find the matching picture on the next page. Whoever is the first to do this puts one of his 'tokens' on the picture. The player who wins more tokens wins a prize.

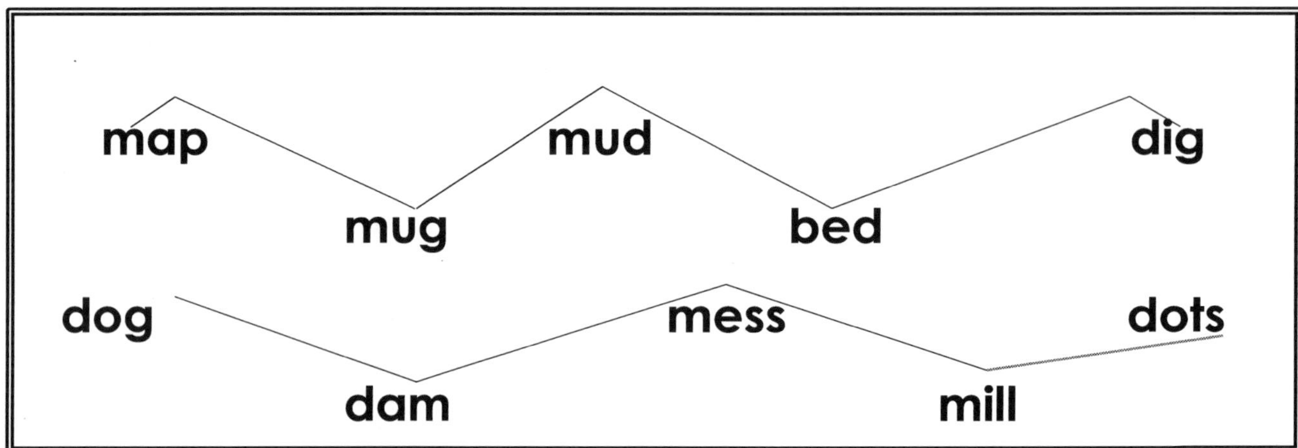

Game 9 – The Magic Bed Spell

A Wickedly Wily Word Reading Game

- Spell the word 'bed' with letter cards supplied (see pages 55 and 101).
- Help your child read it and point out how the word looks a bit like a bed.
- Mix up the letters. Ask your child to 'make' the *bed* again.
- Put your fists together with your thumbs tucked inside. Raise your index fingers to 'make' the ends of a bed. Ask your child to make a bed this way.
- Ask your child to point to the hand that says /b/ and the hand that says /d/. Whenever your child is confused about these letters, just remind her to make a bed in this way.

Game 8 – Hunt High and Low pictures

Game 10 – Coughing Rockets

☺ *Comic Mnemonic Games*

- Show your child the mnemonics for the letters **r** and **c** on the next page.
- Read the stories. Ask questions about the *shape* and *sound* of each letter.
- When pronouncing the /r/ sound, it may be easier to think of the sound as a long /errrrrr/. Help your child say /er/, not /ruh/; and to say /c/, not /cuh/.
- Ask 'why' questions about the details in the pictures: 'Why does this letter look like a little rocket? Why are there crumbs coming out of the girl's mouth?'
- Point to letters in the picture and the text and ask, 'What does this letter say?'

Game 11 – Talking Letters

A Lickety-Split Letter-Sound Game

- Point to the box below, and explain that all the letters are inside a room 'talking' on their phones (*saying their sounds*).
- Take turns making the letters 'talk' (say their sounds), from left to right, line by line. Then, take turns to make the letters 'talk' faster.
- If an error is made, it becomes the other player's turn.

c m r s n p o t e l i d

r c g r b e d c n r m l

Game 10 – Coughing Rockets

Game 12 – Cough and Roar

☺ *A Comic Mnemonic Game*

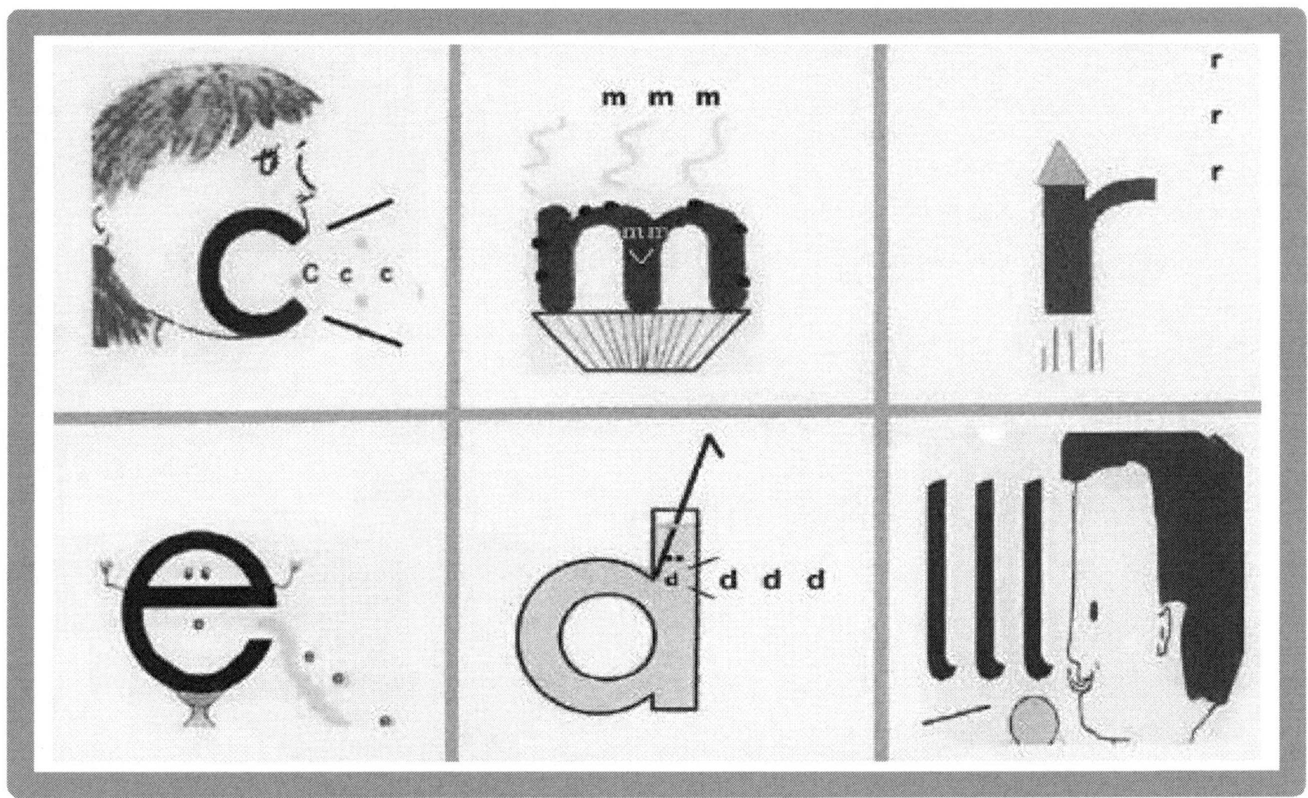

- Ask, 'In the box above, can you find the letter that says: (/l/, /e/, /m/, /d/, /r/, /c/)?'
- Ask, 'Can you find the letter that is shaped like -- (a muffin, a rocket, an egg, a coughing mouth, a long, licking tongue, a donut stuck to a drink)?'
- Point to letters and ask, 'What sound does this letter make?'
- Or ask, 'What sound does the letter that looks like (a long tongue, a fat egg, a bumpy muffin, a donut stuck to a drink, a roaring rocket, a curly, coughing mouth) make?' Tell your child how clever she or he is.
- Let your child test *you* on the shapes and sounds of these letters.
- Keep your child on the alert by making the occasional mistake.

Game 13 – Blast Off!

❖ *A Mind-Bending Sound Blending Game*

- Show your child the rocket on the next page, and tell your child he will be able to make it 'Blast Off' by reading the words from the base to the top.
- Point to the word *cat*, and help your child read the first 2-letter part /ca/.
- When he can read the /ca/ sound well, ask him to slide it into the final /t/ sound. Help him read the next word in the same way.
- When he reaches the top, together count down: 'Five, four, three, two, one . . . Blast Off!' Play the game until your child can read the words easily. Award treats.

Game 14 – Red Rocket Match

A Wickedly Wily Word Reading Game

- Ask your child to read the first word at the bottom of the rocket (next page.)
- Give help as needed and congratulate.
- Ask, 'Can you find the matching picture for that word?'
- If correct, let him put a token on top of the picture.
- When your child has read all the words, award a treat for each token he won.

Game 13 – Blast Off!

cut
ram
cub
rod
cap
rat
cob
red
cat

Lower Case Letter Cards

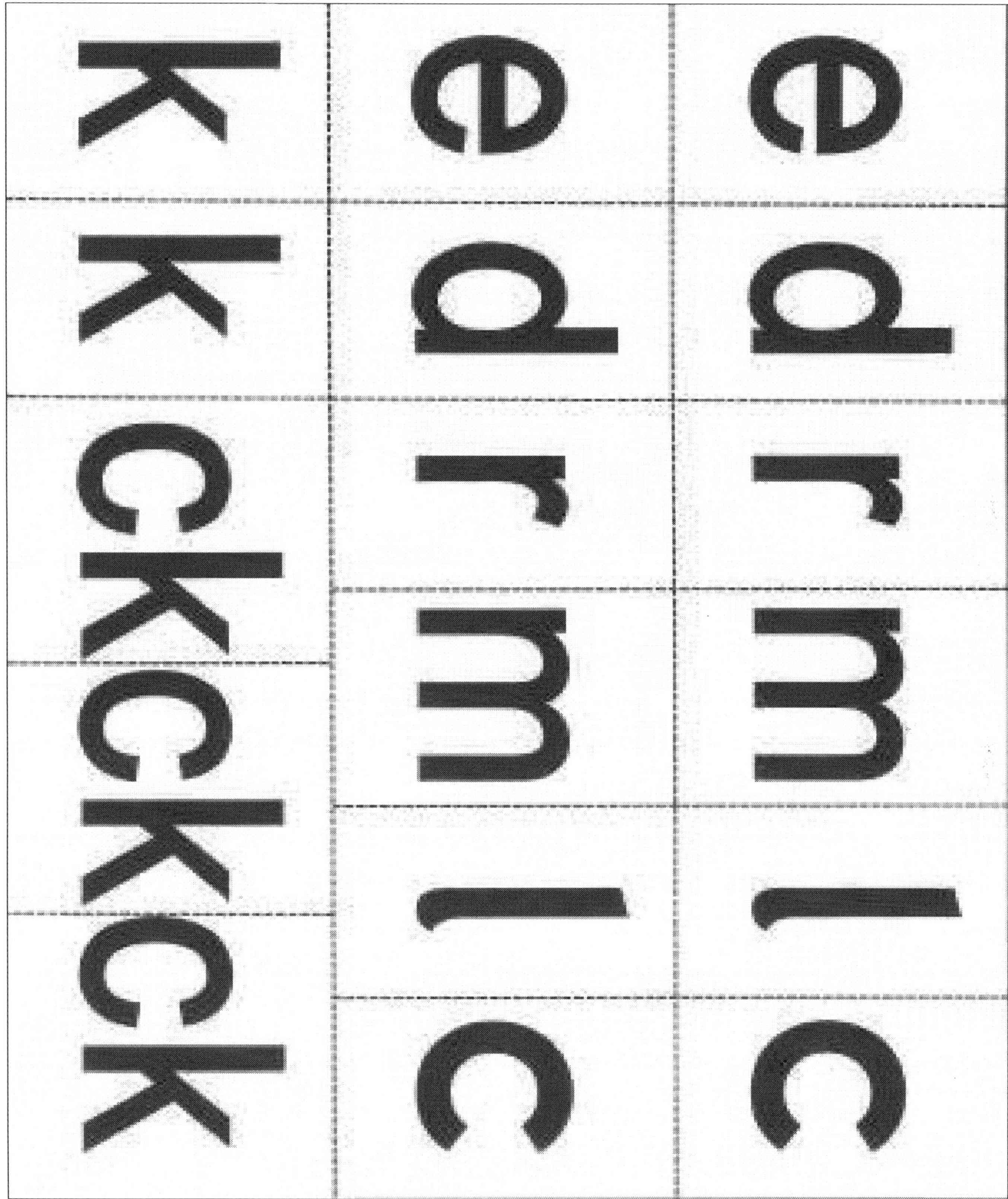

Left intentionally blank for Lower Case Letter Cards on reverse

Game 15 – Kicking and Coughing

☺ *A Comic Mnemonic Game*

- Show your child the **k** picture above and read the mini-story.
- Point to the boy's odd kicking, **k**-shaped mouth. Ask, 'What sound is he making?'
- Ask, 'What sound does the girl who coughs on cake crumbs make?' Together, turn back in the book to find the Comic Mnemonic for the letter **c** (p 97).
- Explain that *both* the letters **c** and **k** make the *same* coughing sound.
- Point to the letter **k** in the picture and in the mini-story, and ask each time, 'What sound does this letter make?'
- Ask, 'Can you find all 15 letters in the box above that make the /c/ sound?'
- Congratulate your child excitedly. Ask him or her to join in with you while you kick and cough and make lots of coughing sounds: /c/, /k/, /c/, /k/.

Game 16 – Cake Crumbs

📖*A Wickedly Wily Word Reading Game*

- Ask your child if he can follow the trail of cake crumbs below, reading the words as he goes to find a secret reward at the end (a kiss).

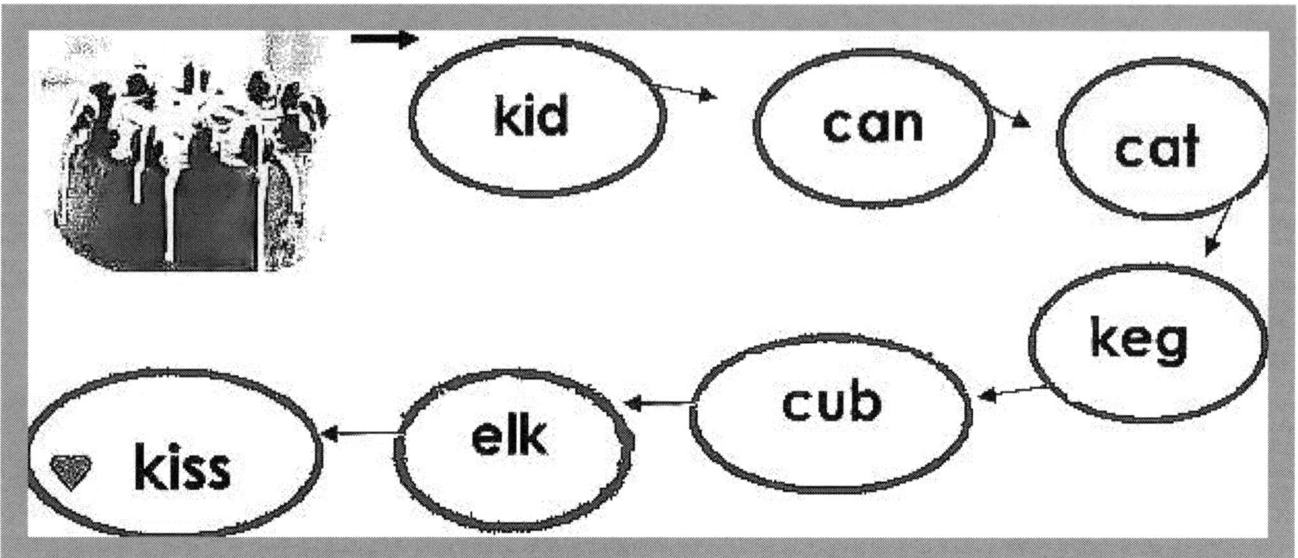

Game 17 – Clever Kids

☺ *A Comic Mnemonic Game*

- The illustration on the next page explains that the letters **c** and **k**, and the letter combination **ck** *all* make the *same* sound.
- Read the mini-story while pointing to letters indicated by the arrows: the girl's **c**-shaped mouth, the boy's **k**-shaped mouth, and the letter combination **ck.**
- Point to letters **c**, **k** and **ck**, in turn, and ask, 'What sound does this letter make? And this one? And these two letters together?'
- Ask, 'How many sounds do **c** and **k** make when together?' (Answer: Just ONE)

- Point to the letters **ck** in the word *sock*, and ask, 'So what do these two letters say again?' Point to the *cat*, *sock*, and *kiss* pictures. See if your child can read the words.
- Point to any of the target letters or letter combinations (**c**, **k**, and **ck**) in the picture or text, and ask for each one, 'What does this say?'
- Point to other letters once in a while to see if your child notices!

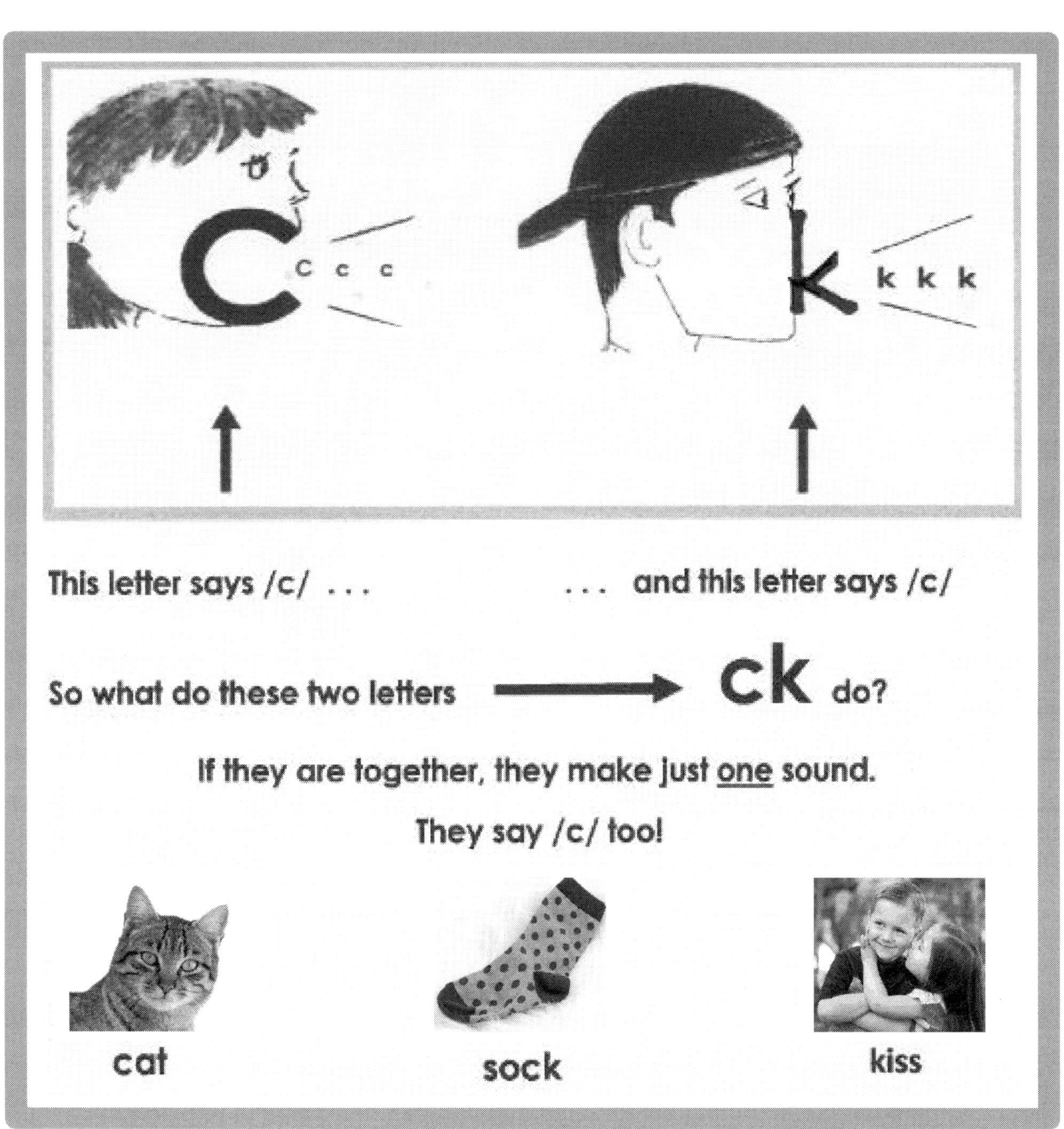

Game 18 – Lucky Duck ♥

❖ *A Mind-Bending Sound Blending Game*

- Show your child the next page. Explain that the duck at the start has lost her pond. And her mate! (Point to the picture at the end.)
- Ask, 'Shall we help her? She has to find her way past all these obstacles (point to the 2-letter word parts) by saying their sounds to get there.'
- Point to /du/ and ask, 'What does this one say?' Help your child sound out /d/+/u/, and blend the sounds to say/du/, as heard in the word *duck*.
- If she does not say the sound right away, just ask 'Does it say /du/?'
- Celebrate when the duck finds the pond, and her mate. Give your child a hug.

Game 19 – Super Two

❖ *A Mind-Bending Sound Blending Game*

This game focuses on beginning consonant blends involving the letters **r, l, c, k.** Have some lower case letter cards on hand (see pp 21, 55, and 101).

- Give your child *just three letters*; include the 2 letters needed to make the blend.
- Warn your child that you are going to say a sound, and he should listen SUPER carefully for *two* sounds.
- Ask, 'Are you ready? Pronounce any of the following: **fr** **tr** **sl** **dr** **sk** **cr** **cl** **st**. Draw out the 2 sounds as much as you can.
- Ask, 'What is the 1st sound you hear? And the 2nd?' Help your child select the correct two letters (from the three letters he has) to make the blend.
- Each time, reward with 2 hugs, 2 kisses, or 2 treats.

du...ki...

li...de...so...

.ki...ro...be..

..mu..lu..se..

.si...pon..

Game 20 – Something to Quack About

- Take turns sounding the word parts above and trying to spell a word by adding the letters **ck.** (Have letters ck on hand from page 101) If a real word is made, the player wins a token (button or coin).
- The player with more tokens at the end of the trail QUACKs loudly for a treat.

Game 21 – The *Flip-Flap* reader instructions

The pages of the Flip-Flap reader follow. Here's what to do:

PAGE 1 – (top half of page):

- First, cover the lower half of the page.
- Tell your child, 'Because you are such a clever reader, you are ready for *another* little book of your own to read!' Ask, 'What is its name?'
- Show your child the book's cover page (the top half of the page). Point underneath to every letter in the two words, as together, you slowly sound out and read the title: *F l i p – F l a p*. (Make the blended sound /fl/ for your child to copy). Discuss the pictures; help your child read the words underneath.

PAGE 1 – (lower half of page):

- Say, 'Let's see what comes next.' Uncover the lower half of the page.
- Point out the letters **l e m d r c k ck** at the top of the first reader page. Ask your child to tell you what sound each of these letters, or letter combinations, make.
- Cover the pictures, and then follow these three steps:
  1) Help your child sound out each of the words in 2 parts: /du/+/ck/, /li/+/ck/, /ro/+/ck/, /ki/+/ck/. Praise him or her warmly after each word.
  2) Now go back, and help your child read the words again until he can read all the words easily. Be sure to tell your child how clever he is.
  3) Next, reveal the pictures. As your child reads each word once more, ask, 'Can you find the matching picture?' Praise highly.

PAGES 2 – 5:

For each half-page, cover the pictures and follow the three steps outlined above.

During the process of reading with your child, explain the following:

Two- Syllable Words:

Some 2-syllable words that appear are *rocket, muffin, rabbit*. Dotted, vertical lines divide these words into syllables. These lines show the 2 parts your child should read separately: *rock – et, muf – fin*, etc.

Sentences:

These appear later on in the reader. Explain these conventions -

1) Big, important letters (*called capitals*) are used at the beginning of a sentence.
2) A *period* (or *full stop*) shows where a sentence ends.
3) An *exclamation mark* means someone is excited, or shouting.

Tricky Words are underlined:

Tell your child that these words do not make sense when sounded out the normal way. (Your child might pronounce the word has as /hass/, for example.) On the last cover page of the booklet, your child can see how this word should have been spelled if it followed the normal sounding out rules.

On the last three pages of the reader:

On the final three pages (2 story pages + back cover), it is not necessary to hide the pictures. Let your child study the pictures after reading each sentence. The pictures are arranged in order, matching the sequence of the story.

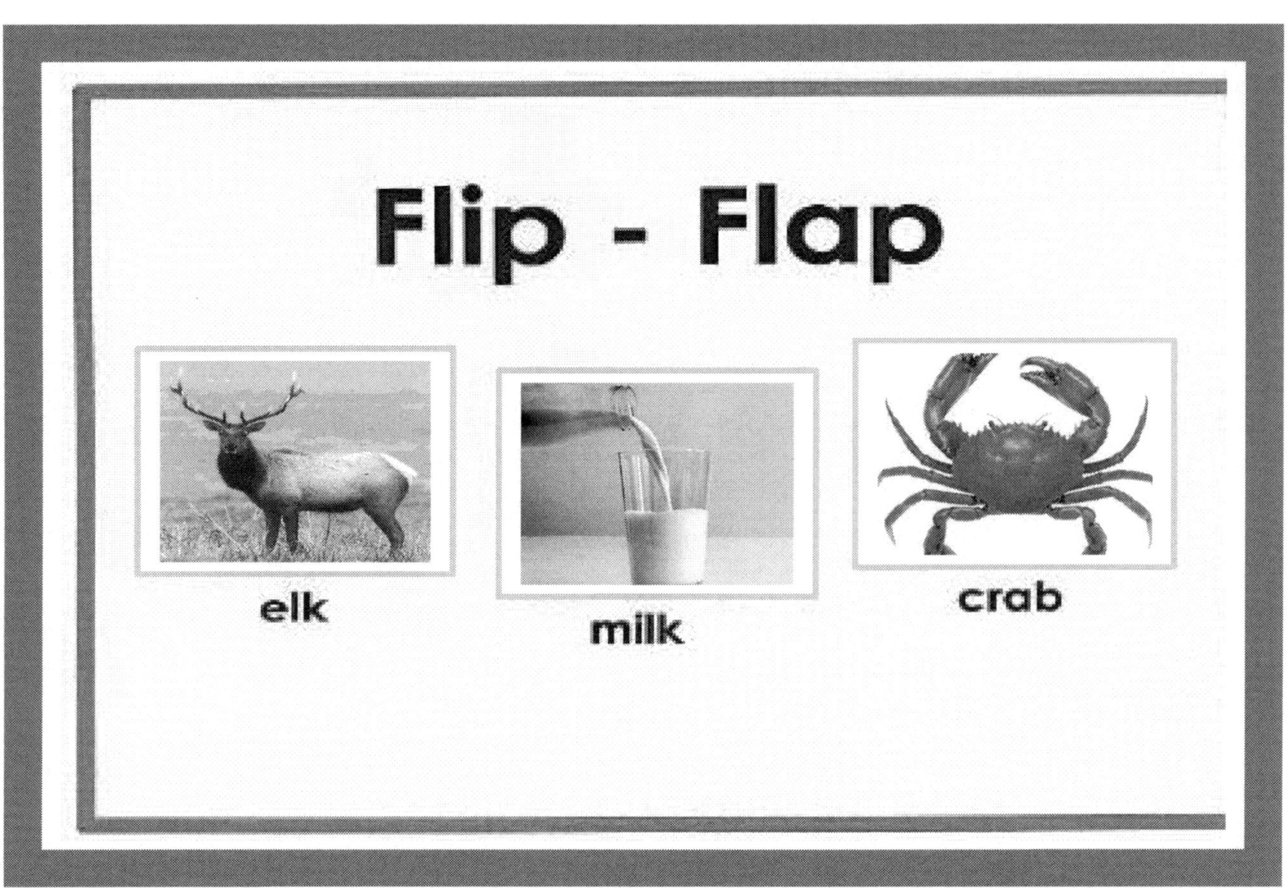

l e m d r c k ck

duck

lick

rock

kick

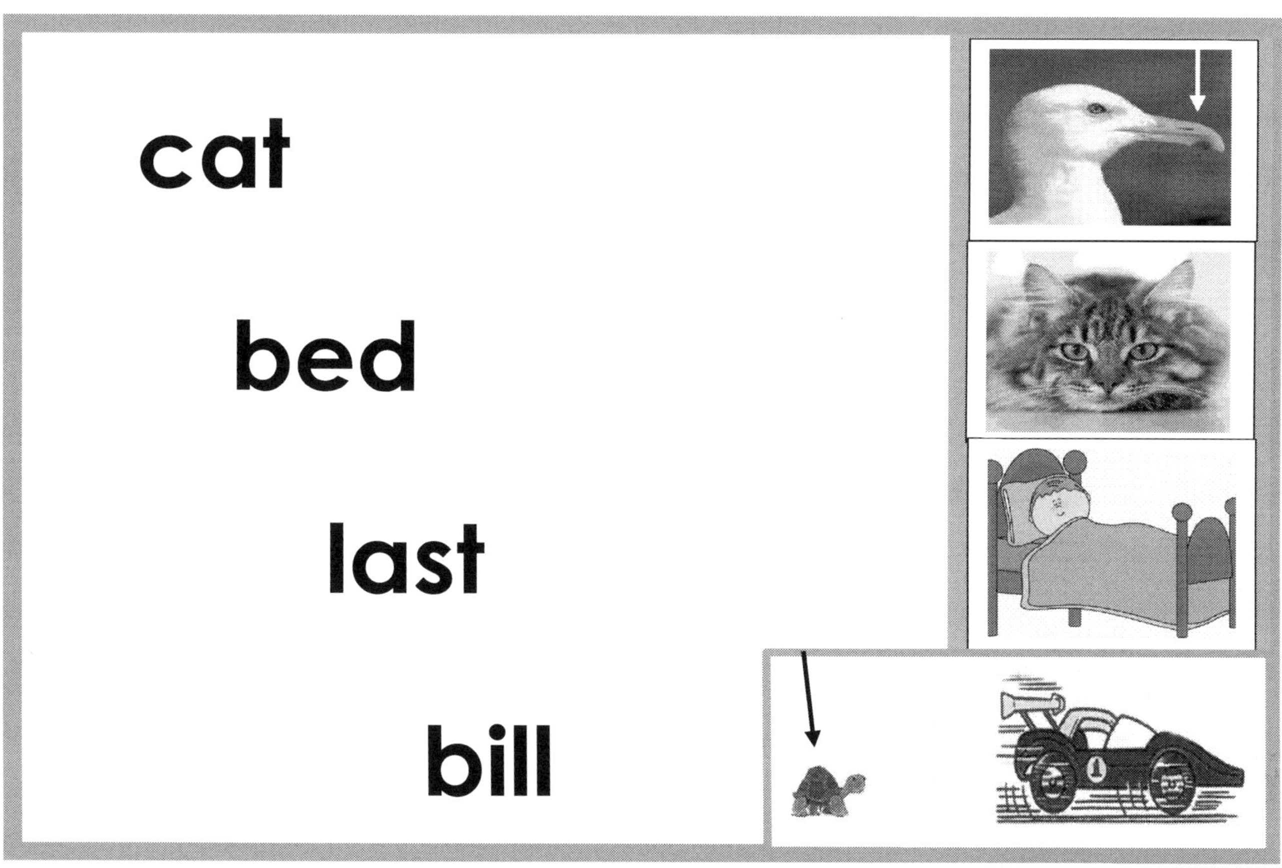
cat
bed
last
bill

nest
milk
tusk
tent

a skunk

a rocket

a muffin

a rabbit

A dog begs.

It is a red drink.

It can cut.

A dog digs.

Meg is sick in bed.

A duck sits.

eggs in a nest

clams and a crab

a bucket and a mop

A kitten sits.

A cub runs.

A dog hugs a cat.

A frog has a stick.

Tom has a drill.

Ella has a cap.

Mick digs in sand.

'Mick! Help!'

A man and <u>his</u> dog

run <u>to</u> help.

Mick still digs . . .

Tricky Words in this Book

is	**has**	**his**	**to**
(iz)	(haz)	(hiz)	(too)

Chapter 4

j ee w oo z y

Contents

zoo
yak
roo
moose
zebra
goose
Paste the segment with the word moose here.
Paste the segment with the word zebra here.
Paste the segment with the word goose here.
goose
zebra
moose

Chapter 4

Welcome to Book 4 which introduces six new letters or letter combinations:

j ee w oo z y,

and their sounds: /j/, /ee/, /w/, /oo/, / z/, /y/.

Here's how to pronounce the six new sounds:

/**j**/ - As in the word *jump*. Keep the sound short; /j/, not /juh/.

/**ee**/ - As in the words *eel* and *teeth*. The sound continues - /eeeee/.

/**w**/ - First sound in the word *wave*. Keep the sound short; /w/, not /wuh/.

/**oo**/ - As heard in the word *boo*. The sound continues - /ooooo/.

/**z**/ - First sound heard in the word *zoo*. The sound continues – /zzzzzzzz/.

/**y**/ - First sound in the word *yippee*. Keep the sound short; /y/, not /yuh/.

Using the Comic Mnemonics

In this chapter, as in chapter 3, the mnemonic pictures and mini-stories are combined with the games. All you need to do is play the games in the sequence they appear. Try to play the games for about 20 – 25 minutes a day. Remember, even if you are referring to a letter shape, refer to it by *sound*, not its name.

A Suggested 7-Day Plan

The following 7-Day Plan is simply a suggestion. Do not worry if you miss a day and fall behind. You can always replay the games at any point as a way to review any material that your child may have forgotten.

A Suggested 7-Day Plan

Day

1 Play Games 1, 2 and 3 introducing the letter **j** and the letters **ee**.

2 Repeat Game 3. Play Games 4 and 5 introducing the letter **w**.

3 Play Game 5 again. Play Games 6, 7 and 8 introducing the letters **oo**, **z** and **y**.

4 Play Game 9. Read the *Peek-A-Boo* reader together once.

5 Repeat Game 9. Read the *Peek-A-Boo* reader once more and have your child continue to read it until fluent.

6 Play Game 10. Help your child read the 1, 2, 3 – *Swim in the Pool* reader.

7 Continue to help your child read both readers until your child is fluent and enjoys reading them to family and friends.

Game 1 – Jack-in-the Box

☺ *A Comic Mnemonic Game*

Show your child the mnemonic picture below for the sound /j/. Discuss what a Jack-in-the Box is: a toy where the lid on the top of the box is latched, a handle is turned to play music, the latch releases, the lid pops open, and the 'Jack' in the box jumps out.

- Read the mini-story with animation. Ask, 'Who is Jack?' (a Jack-in-the-box)
- Ask, 'Why doesn't Jack want to go back in the box?' (he *loves* to jump)
- 'What keeps Jack in the box?' Explain that the lid has a latch that keeps it closed.
- Ask, 'What happens when the lid pops open?' (Jack jumps out)
- Ask, 'What happy noise does Jack make when he's jumping?' (/j/ /j/ /j/)
- Ask, '*Why* does this letter say /j/? (this is his happy jumping noise)
- Point to any letter **j** in the picture or text, and ask, 'What does this *say*?'
- Ask your child to point to all the letters that say /j/ making the sound each time.

Game 2 – Jack and Jill Went Up the Hill

A Wickedly Wily Word Reading Game

- On the next page are two word lists. Two players, 'Jack and Jill', climb up a hill: they take turns to go up the hill by sounding out and reading words one by one, starting from the bottom of their lists. * For a more interactive game version, see below.
- When they reach the top of the 'hill' (their list), players must find pictures that match their words on this page below. Each time they find a matching picture, a player leaves his token (a coin or a button) on top of his word.
- The first player to find matching pictures for *all* his words is the winner.
- Reward the winner with a refreshing drink or special treat.

Game 2 – *Jack and Jill* words

jet	jam
junk	Jack
jump	Jill
jog	jug

Game 3 – Can You See Happy Me?

☺ *A Comic Mnemonic Game*

Look! Can you see?
Two letters by the
name of '**e**'
Together is where
they want to be
Can you hear their
sound of glee?
Hee-hee - /ee/ /ee/

- Read the mini-story above, and point out the two **e**'s together in the picture.
- Point to them again, and ask, 'What do these *two* letters look like? (teeth)
- Ask, 'When these two letters get together they make a *new* happy, laughing sound. What is it?'(/ee/) 'What was that again?' (/ee/)
- Ask your child to find all the letter combinations that say /ee/ in the picture and the text, and to say their sound each time.
- Give your child two letter **e** cards (from page 101). Place them spaced apart.
- Point to each one in turn, and ask, 'What does this letter say?' (/e/ as in egg)
- Ask your child to push the two letters *together* and tell you what *new* sound they make now. Repeat this exercise several times, and congratulate.
- Ask, '***Why*** do these 2 letters say /ee/?'(they are laughing and happy to be together) If necessary, read the mini-story again to find out why.

Game 4 – Wavy Waves

☺ *A Comic Mnemonic Game*

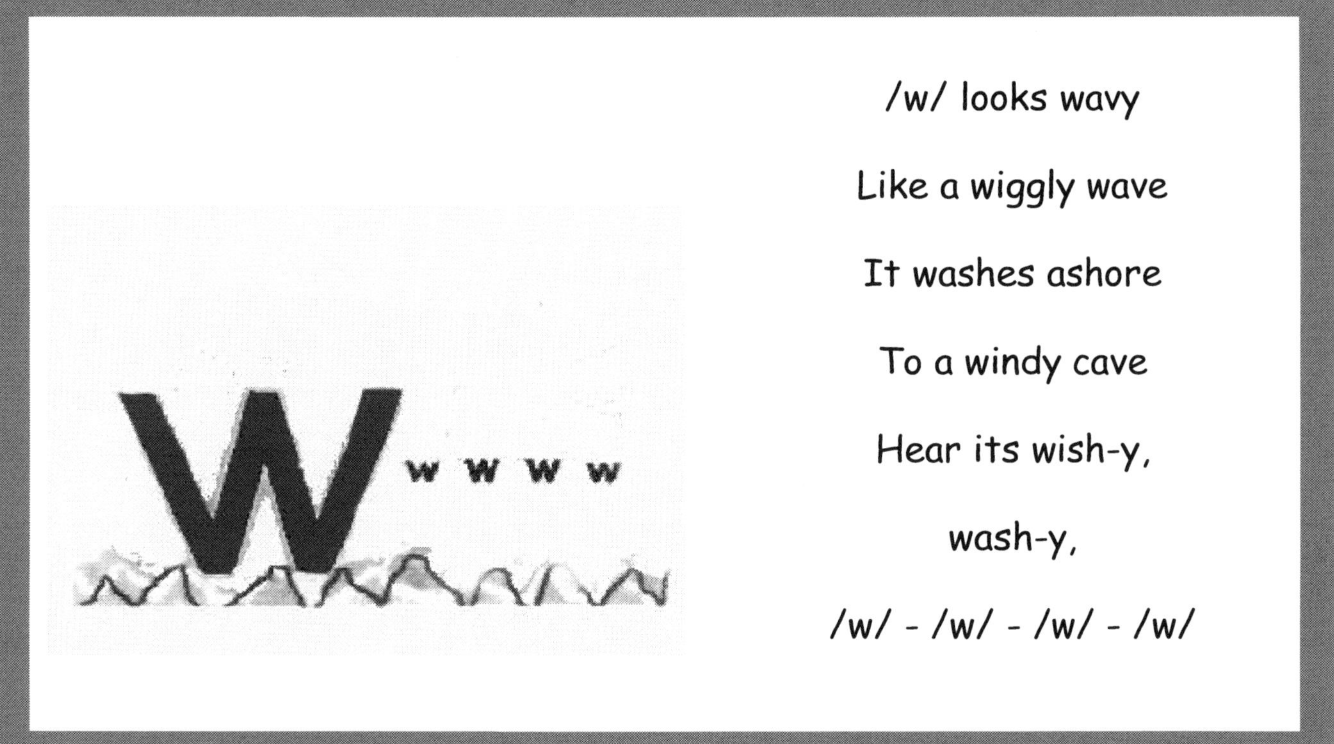

- Read the mini-story above to your child in a rhythmic voice.
- Ask, 'What does this letter look like? (a wiggly wave)
- Point to the letter **w** in the picture. Ask, 'What sound does this letter make?' (/w/, not /wuh/)
- Ask your child to repeat the sound in a steady rhythm like the wishy, washy sound of waves. (/w/ /w/ /w/ /w/) Praise enthusiastically.
- Ask your child to find all the letters in the picture and the mini-story that say /w/, and pronounce their sound three times on each occasion.
- Ask, '*Why* does this letter say /w/?' (it enjoys making a wishy-washy noise like waves)
- PRAISE your child highly throughout the game.

Game 5 – Wiggly Eel ✋

📖 *A Wickedly Wily Word Reading Game*

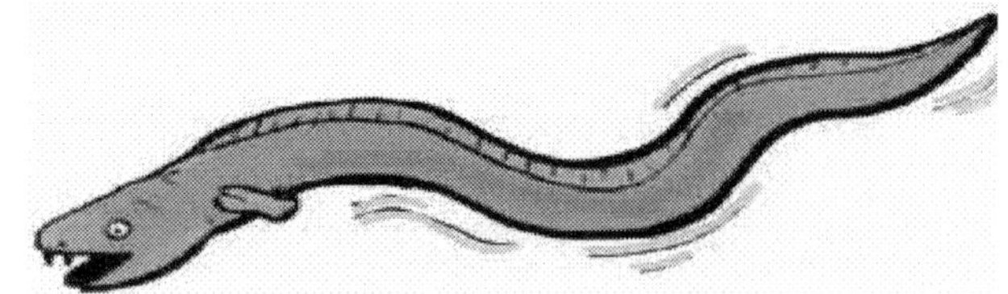

- Play this game using the next page just as it is. Or see an alternative below.*
- Cover everything on the next page except the first word.
- Have your child start the game by helping him to sound out the word in two parts, /ee/ + /l/. (Or later, /wi + /g/, /s/ + /ee/, /wa/ + /g/,/ b/ + /ee/, /we/ + / t/.)
- Once he succeeds, uncover the next segment to reveal the picture of the eel.
- Point to the picture and ask, 'Were you right?' Congratulate him enthusiastically.
- Uncover the next segment and help him sound out the next word (/wi/ + /g/).
- Once he can read the word, uncover the next segment to reveal the picture of a girl wearing a wig. Point to the wig on the girl and ask, 'Were you right? Is this a wig?'
- If your child was not correct, it becomes the other player's turn who must start from the beginning. (When it is your turn, make mistakes so your child will have more turns.)
- The winner must reach the tail of the eel without making any mistakes.
- He should then receive a really – r**eel**y - wonderful treat!

Game 5 – Wiggly Eel ✋

Game 6 – Yack, Zack, Zoom

☺ *A Comic Mnemonic Game*

- Show your child the next page and read each mini-story twice over, in turn.
- Pronounce the /oo/ sound, in a soft, spooky voice, a long, continuous sound.
- Pronounce the /z/ sound in a lazy, droning voice, letting the /zzz/ sound continue.
- Pronounce the /y/ sound in a happy, excited voice; a short /y/ sound, not /yuh/.
- Ask questions about the letter shapes:

  'Where are the two letters that look like the eyes of a spooky ghost? Can you find the letter that looks like a zig-zaggy line zooming lazily along? Where is the letter that looks like it has its arms up yelling yippee?'
- Point to letters in the pictures or text and ask, 'What sound does this letter (do these two letters) say?'
- Encourage your child to make these sounds in the appropriate voices – spooky, droning, or excited.

Game 7 – Jeewoozy Jumble

A Lickety-Split Letter-Sound Game

- Ask your child to find letters that say: /j/ /ee/ /w/ /oo/ /z/ /y/ in the box below.
- Point to letters and letter combinations at random and ask, 'What does this say?'

Game 6 – Yack, Zack, Zoom

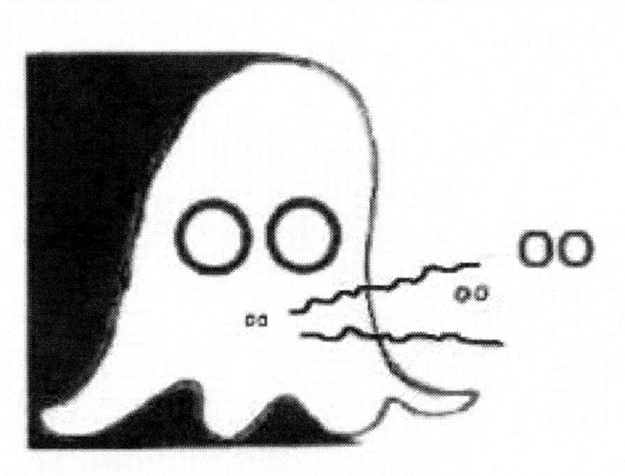

'/oo/ - /oo/ -/oo/'

This spooky ghost

Wants to scare you

So he says,

'/oo/ - /oo/ - /oo/ - boo !'

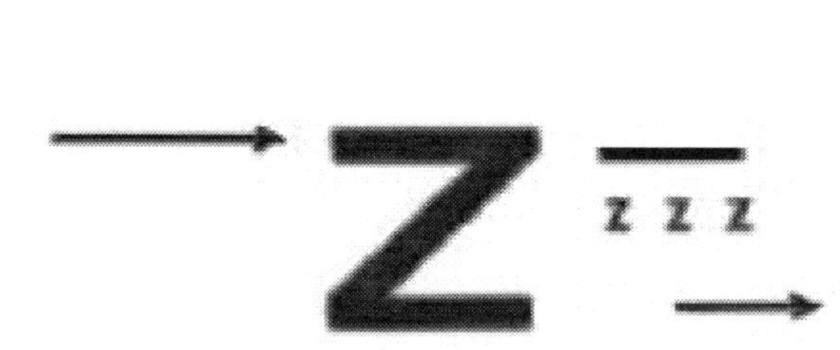

Here is /zzz/

A zig-zaggy line

Can you hear his

/zzz/

As he zips, zaps and

Zooms along fine?

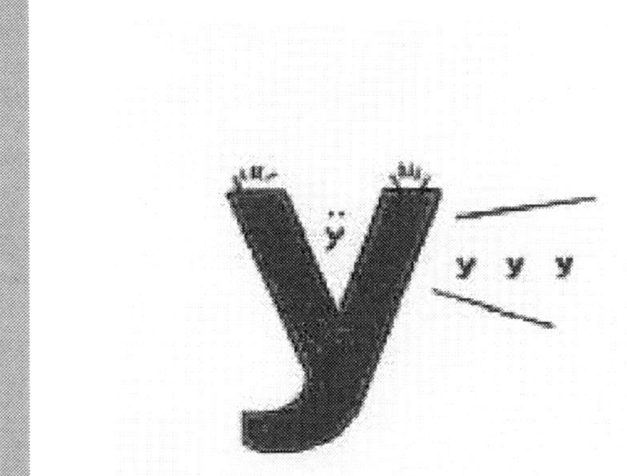

/y/ as you can see

Has both arms up

And he yips,

'/y/ - /y/ - /y/ -

Yippee !'

Game 8 – Zigzag Zoo 🖐

📖 A Wickedly Wily Word Reading Game

- Play this game using the facing page just as it is.
- Cover everything except the first word. Help your child read the word, (/z/ +/oo/).
- Praise and uncover another segment of the zigzag to reveal the picture.
- Was your child correct? Ask, 'What was the word again? Can you see that word in the picture? What does it say?'
- Reveal another segment of the zigzag to see the next word. Ask, 'Can I have a turn now?' Attempt to read the word saying, instead of *yak*, perhaps *yuck*.
- Uncover the picture and admit that you made an error and say, 'Now it's your turn again but we have to start from the beginning!' Cover up the page again and see how far your child can read the words without error.

🖐 **- see page xiii**

Game 8 – *Zigzag Zoo*

zoo	 Glue the segment with the word *yak* here.
yak	 Glue the segment with the word *roo* here.
roo	 Glue the segment with the word *moose* here.
moose	 Glue the segment with the word *zebra* here.
zebra	 Glue the segment with the word *goose* here.
goose	 **FEEDING TIME!**

Game 9 – Green Spoons

📖 *A Wickedly Wily Word Reading Game*

- Let your child choose a numbered slip from 1 to 6; then locate the number below.
- To practise reading words with initial consonant blends: help your child read all 4 words in each line. To begin with, you can make the sound of the initial 2-letter blend for your child to copy (/sp/ /tr/ /gr/ /tw/...).
- Then when fluent, ask, 'Can you find the word that matches the picture?' Reward.

1) spoon spit spill speed	
2) truck tree trick trip	
3) grab grip green grass	
4) twin twit tweet twig	
5) slip sleep slam slug	
6) cliff club clap clam	

Tricky Words

The concept of *Tricky Words* (words not easy to sound out) was introduced in Chapter 3. Because there are a few more irregularly spelled words included in the two reading booklets that follow (Games 10 and 11), the topic arises again.

The *majority* of words are easy to sound out It's a common myth that English spellings are highly irregular. The truth is, computer studies show that the majority of words (*up to 80%)* in the English language are regularly spelled. They follow spelling rules that make them easy to sound out and straightforward to read. And yet, the English language has a reputation for being more irregularly spelled than many other languages.

The frequency of Tricky Words There is a reason for this view. It is the high frequency of commonly used words, some of which are irregularly spelled, that create this impression. Common words such as - *of, to, is, was, I, his* - do not follow the normal sounding out rules. Further adding to the impression of irregularity, *one half* of all the English words seen in print consist of just one hundred, frequently used, words. And *some of these are* spelled irregularly.

But how many? Examination reveals that of these one hundred words, only about one third are strictly irregular. In fact, *more than two thirds* of these 100 frequently used words are spelled regularly. They are easy to sound out, and their spelling patterns follow rules.

This is why it makes sense that early reading instruction should rely, *first and foremost,* on a sounding out approach. A letter-to-sound translation approach gives your child the most useful strategy, a reading strategy that will work most of the time.

However, once your child has firmly grasped the idea that, in order to read, one must sound out all the letters in a word, it is then safe to introduce him to some of the most highly occurring, irregularly spelled words.

Frequently occurring Tricky Words What are these words? Ranked in order of frequency, the following 14 irregularly spelled words are among the first 25 words that make up *one third of all printed material*:

the of to is you he was are as his they I be have

After encountering these frequently used words just a few times, your child will begin to recognize them. Furthermore, evidence shows your child will learn to recognize them *much faster* than a child who has not learned any letter-sound relationships. With nearly all of the 14 words above, knowing some letter-to-sound associations will make it easier to recognize them. Before your child knows *all* the 44 letter-sound associations, however, here are some extra tips to help your child tackle the reading of these words.

Six Terrific Tips to Tackle Tricky Words

1) 'Sound Out

Have your child sound out the letters in a Tricky Word using his usual letter-to-sound translation approach. Why? This way your child will notice immediately that there is something odd about the word. [The word *was*, sounded out in the usual way, would produce the word /wasss/ (to rhyme with the word *mass)]*. Similarly, the word *is*, would sound like */isss/* (to rhyme with *hiss*.)

2) 'Wonder

You can both now wonder, 'That's silly, isn't it? There is no such word as *wasss*, is there?'

3) 'Watch Out!

After deciding that the word does not exist, warn your child, 'Uh-oh! This must be one of those Tricky Words!' Explain, 'This word is a bit naughty. And, sneaky! It doesn't want to follow the rules. It wants to *trick* you! So, watch out!'

4) 'Tricky Word' Alert

In these materials, the first time a tricky word appears in a reader, it will be underlined. In addition, it will also be listed on the back cover of the book. Point out the Tricky Word symbol (a sneaky-looking cat) on the back cover of the book. Together, look to see if the word you are wondering about is listed there.

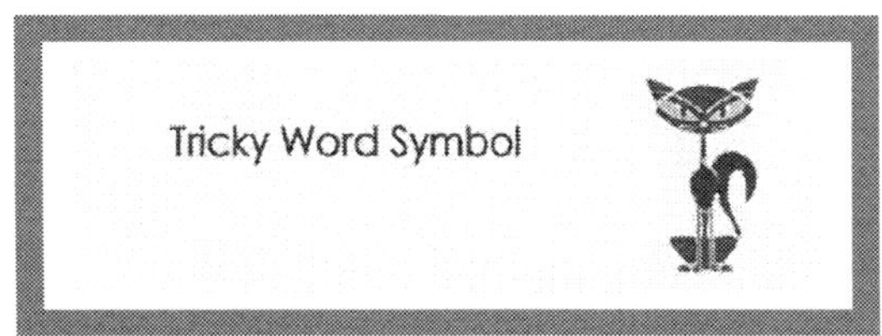

5) What Does the Word *Really* Say?

Read the phrase or sentence again, pronouncing the tricky word according to normal rules. For example, 'It /isss/ cool in the pool.' Point to the word and explain, 'This word says /isss/, but there is no such word is there? I wonder what it *really* says?' (Often the sound of the word according to phonic rules is so similar to the way the actual word is pronounced, it is the best clue when determining what the word might be.)

Whether your child guesses what the word says or not, look at the back cover of the book together and locate the word. To see how it is really pronounced, point to the word in brackets that appears underneath. In the case of the word *is*, it is /iz/. The way to pronounce the words is /iz/.

6) Celebrate Not Being Tricked

Ask your child to confirm what the word says, and then exclaim how clever your child is. Don't miss out this step because children really enjoy this part. Exclaim, 'Well done! That word tried to trick you, didn't it? But YOU weren't tricked! It didn't trick YOU! Clever you!'

To review, the Six Terrific Tips to Tackle Tricky Words are:

1) Sound Out

2) Wonder

3) Watch Out!

4) Tricky Word Alert

5) What Does the Word *Really* Say?

6) Celebrate Not Being Tricked

Game 10 – *Peek-A-Boo* reader instructions

COVER PAGE:

- Show your child the cover of the *Peek-a-Boo* reader on the top half of the next page.
- Say, 'You are reading so well now, you are ready for another little book of your own! 'What is the name of this book?'
- Help your child sound out and read the title. (Remind your child that people's names as well as names of books, are capitalized.)
- Discuss the pictures and help your child sound out and read the three words: *wet, peek, jump*: /we/ + /t/, /p/ + /ee/ /k/, /ju/ +/m/ /p/.)

PAGE ONE:

- Direct your child's attention to the bottom half of the page. *Cover up the pictures with blank paper.*
- Point to the series of letters. Explain that this book is all about those letter-sounds. Ask, 'Can you tell me what each of these say?' Point to each letter (or letter combination) as your child gives their sounds. Praise highly.
- Help your child read each of the words on the page at least twice, and tell your child frequently how clever he is.
- Then, before your child reads the words once more, say, 'Let's take a peek at the pictures!' Uncover the pictures and see if your child can find the matching picture for each word.
- Praise your child's word and picture matching skills enthusiastically.

FURTHER PAGES:

- When you encounter the word **I,** tell your child that it is actually a big /i/. 'But, when it is big, *and all by itself*, it thinks that it is so important. It proudly swaggers around saying its *name*, 'I, I, I, I . . .'
- When you encounter sentences, point out how they always start with a capital letter and end with a dot (a 'full stop', or a 'period').
- When your child is very speedy at reading the *Peek-a-Boo* reader, and has read it to family and friends, introduce the second reader (Game 11).

Peek-A-Boo
wet
peek
jump

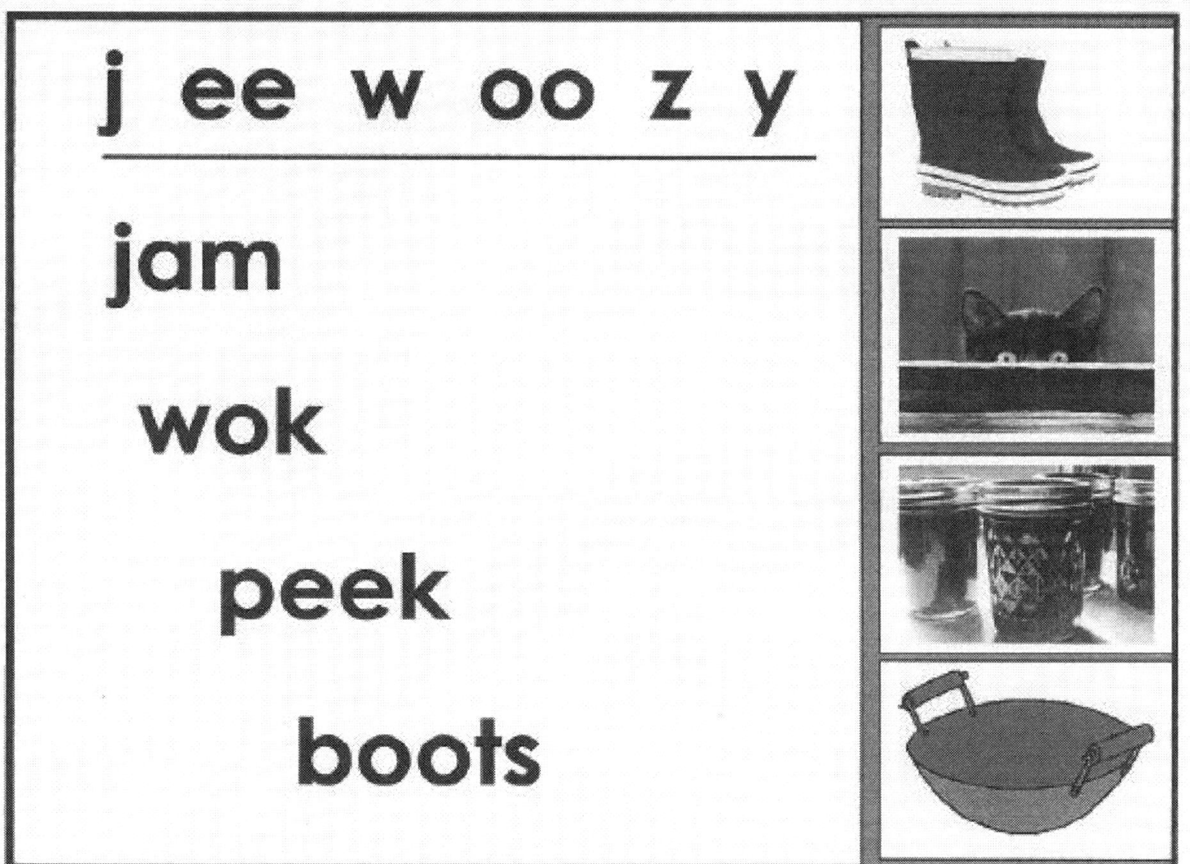
j ee w oo z y
jam
wok
peek
boots

wag

win

wed

wind

hoops

zig|zags

spoons

<u>trees</u>

Jill weeps.

A cat sleeps.

Zac winks.

Ben yells.

a wet web

a green jeep

a steep hill

pink fizz

A jet zooms.

Liz swims.

A cat jumps.

Will <u>speeds</u>.

a tree on a cliff

twins in green

a frog in <u>reeds</u>

kids on a roof

I see feet.

I see seeds.

I see a ba|boon.

I see a rac|coon.

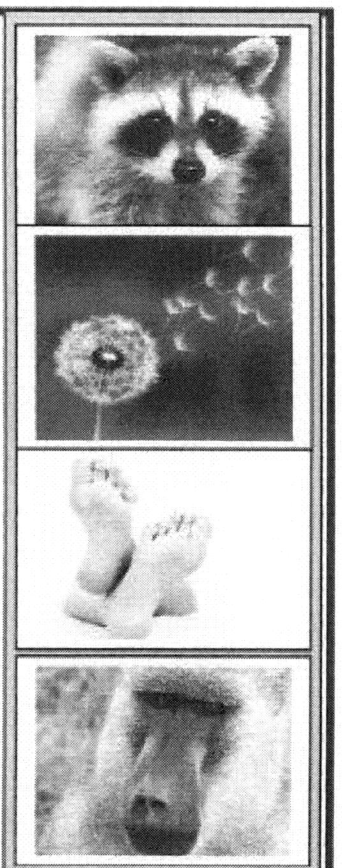

Tricky Words in this Book

trees	speeds	reeds	I	seeds
/treez/	/speedz/	/reedz/	I	/seedz/

Game 11 – *1 2 3: Swim in the Pool* instructions

TITLE PAGE:

- Read the title of the book with your child, pointing out the new, Tricky Word '*the*'. Discuss the picture and what the story might be about.

PAGES:

- After reading the title page, direct attention to the lower half of the page. Point out that there are three sentences. Explain, 'They *all* start with a capital letter and end with a period (full stop).'
- Ask your child to point to the capital letter at the start of each sentence and the period at the end of each sentence.
- Help your child read each of the sentences until he is able to read them without your help. Provide lots of enthusiastic praise and encouragement throughout.

THE 1,2,3 GAME:

- When your child can read each page well, say, 'It's time to play the 1, 2, 3 Game!'
- Point to the numbers and ask, 'Can you point to sentence number 2?' Continue until your child can point to all the sentences by their number.
- Point to the picture below the sentences. Ask, 'When you read the sentences, can you figure out which sentence (sentence #1, 2, or 3) best matches this picture?'
- When your child has selected a number, turn to page J, where the answers for pages A to I are listed. Show your child how to check his answer. Next to the A page, there is a sentence number. Is this the number your child selected?
- Play this game for all the other pages once your child can read a page well.

TRICKY WORDS AND MORE:

- When you encounter underlined, Tricky Words, check the back cover of the booklet. This shows how the words should be spelled if they were following the rules.
- Eventually, let your child practice reading the story on his own. He can check his answers by consulting the answer key on the last page (page J). Praise your child's prowess so highly that he can't wait to show off and read the book to others.

1, 2, 3 – Swim in the Pool

1 The cat sits in the sun.

2 Liz has a drink.

3 Jack, the dog, sleeps.

1, 2, 3?

A

1 Liz is too hot.

2 Liz gets in the cool pool.

3 Jack sits up and sees Liz.

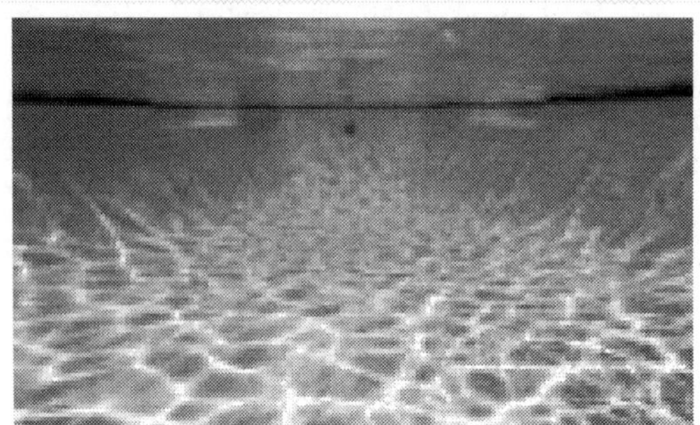

1, 2, 3 ?

B

1 Buzz, the cat, still sleeps.

2 But Jack jumps up.

3 Jack is too hot.

1, 2, 3 ?

C

1 He jumps in the pool to see Liz.

2 Jack yips and yaps.

3 Soon, Liz feels too cool.

1, 2, 3 ?

D

1 Liz sits in the hot sun.

2 Buzz sleeps in the sun.

3 Jack swims and swims.

1, 2, 3 ?

E

1 Soon Jack stands in the sun.

2 He feels too wet. . .

3 Eek! See Jack's trick.

1, 2, 3 ?

F

1 Buzz, the cat, got wet.

2 He <u>is</u> in a bad mood.

3 Liz got wet too.

1, 2, 3 ?

G

1 Liz feeds Buzz.

2 Soon Buzz is well.

3 Liz feeds Jack.

1, 2, 3 ?

H

1 Jack is well too.

2 Soon . . . he is asleep.

3 And Liz has a snooze too.

1, 2, 3 ?

I

Answer Key

A – 2, B - 2, C – 1, D – 1, E – 3, F -3, G – 2, H – 3, I - 2

J

Tricky Words in this Book

the	has	is	He	he	to	snooze
/thu/	/haz/	/iz/	/hee/	/hee/	/too/	/snooz/

Chapter 5

Champ the Chimp

Champ

van

chipmunk

x v qu sh ch th **th**

Contents

Chapter 5

Welcome to Book 5! This chapter introduces two new letters, four new letter combinations, and the sounds they represent:

letter **x** and its sound / ks /, as in the word *box*

letter **v** and its sound / v /, as in the word *van*

letters **qu** and their sound / kw /, as in the word *queen*

letters **sh** and their sound / sh /, as in the word *ship*

letters **ch** and their sound / ch /, as in the word *chick*

letters **th** and their sound / th /, as in the word *thin*

letters **th** and their harder / **th** / sound, as in the word *that*

Using the Comic Mnemonics

In this chapter, similar to the format of Chapter 4, the mnemonic pictures and mini-stories are once again combined with the games. All you need to do is play the games in the sequence they appear. Try to play the games for about 20 – 25 minutes a day, or more if your child is age 5 +. Remember, even if you are referring to a letter shape, refer to it by its *sound*, not its name.

The following plan is simply a suggestion. Do not worry if you miss a day and fall behind. You can always replay the games at any point as a way to review what your child may have forgotten.

A Suggested 7-Day Plan

Day

1 Play games 1 and 2 to introduce and practise the letter-sounds for **x**, **v** and **qu**.

2 Play Games 3 and 4 to introduce and practise the letter combinations **sh** and **ch**.

3 Play Games 5 and 6 to introduce and practise the letter combination **th** as in the word *thin*.

4 Play Game 7 to introduce and practise the letter combination **th** as in the word *that*.

5 Play the word reading games, 8 and 9.

6 Play the word reading games, 10 and 11.

7 Play Game 12 to review the Tricky Words (irregularly spelled words) that your child has been introduced to before. Play Game 13, the *Champ the Chimp* reader. Read the booklet together until your child is able to read it all by himself with fluency and enjoyment.

Game 1 – Tex Mex

☺ *A Comic Mnemonic Game*

Read the mini-story below while pointing to the picture.

Then, ask questions as follows:

- 'Who is Tex - Mex? (a Mexican man)
- 'What does he look like under his Mexican sombrero (hat)?'(an **X**)
- 'Can you repeat the sound he makes 3 times?' (/ks/ /ks/ /ks)
- 'What is the sound like?' (a bit like Mexican maracas (shakers, rattles)

  The sound should be said very quickly, a /k/ sound followed by a /s/ sound,

  like the sound you hear at the end of the word *fox*.)
- Ask, 'Can you point to any letters here in the story that have that 'ex' shape?'
- Ask, 'Can you point to all the letters that look like that in the picture *and* in the story? And each time, can you make their sound?'

For the games below, direct attention to the opposite page.

Game 2 - A Clever Queen

☺ *A Comic Mnemonic Game*

- When you read the first line of the story for **qu**, pronounce the letter *names*: 'A **q** (kew) is always followed by a **u** (you).'
- Ask, 'What queer sound do the queen and her servant make together?' (/kw/)
- Ask, 'Can you make that queer sound again?'
- Ask, 'Can you find those 2 letters in the picture or story? And say their sound?'
- Ask, 'Why is a **q** always followed by a **u**?' (her servant always follows behind)

Game 3 - Valley Vibrations

☺ *A Comic Mnemonic Game*

- Ask, 'What does this letter look like?' (a valley)
- Ask your child to trace the valley shape, starting on the left side of the valley, down into the dip and back up the other side.
- Say the sound '/vvv/' and then exclaim in horror, 'Oh no! I don't like to make the sound of this letter because it goes on and on, and it tickles my lips! '
- Ask, 'Can *you* make that sound? Does it tickle YOUR lips?'
- Ask, 'Can you make the sound last longer? Can you feel the sound vibrate on your lips?'
- Ask, 'Can you find and point to all the valley-shaped letters in the story, and each time, make their vibrating, ticklish sound?'

Game 2 - Clever Queen

☺ *A Comic Mnemonic Game*

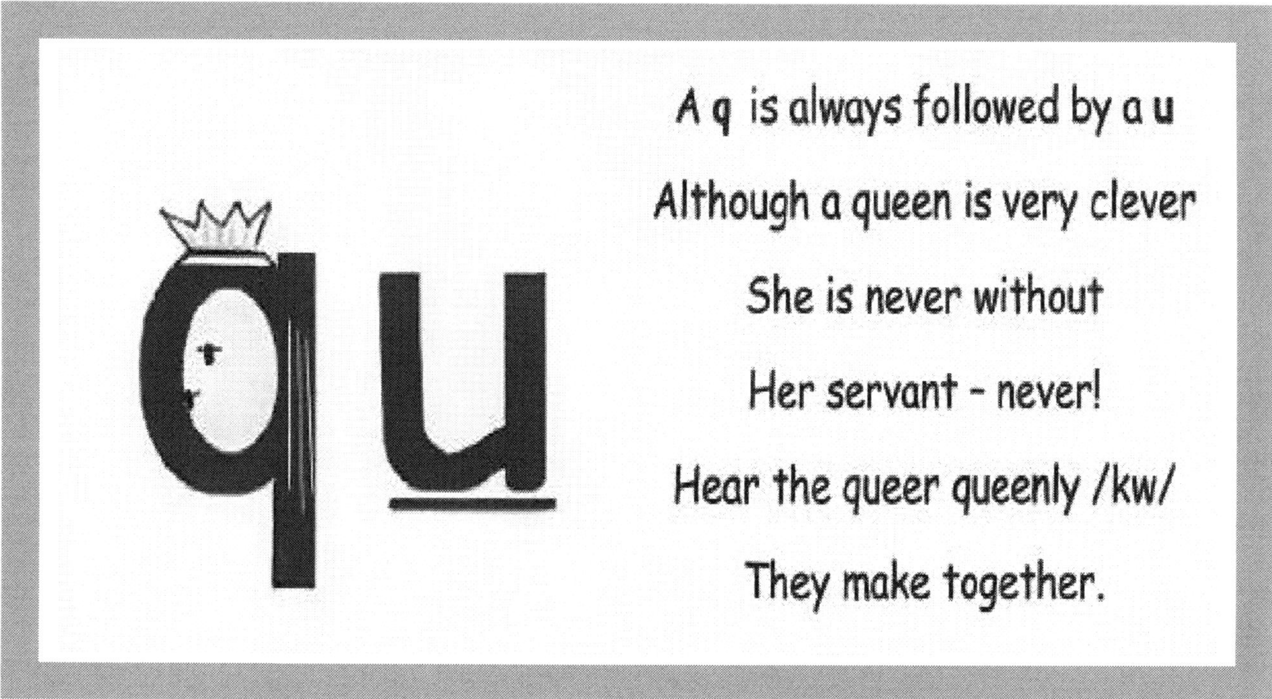

Game 3 – Valley Vibrations

☺ *A Comic Mnemonic Game*

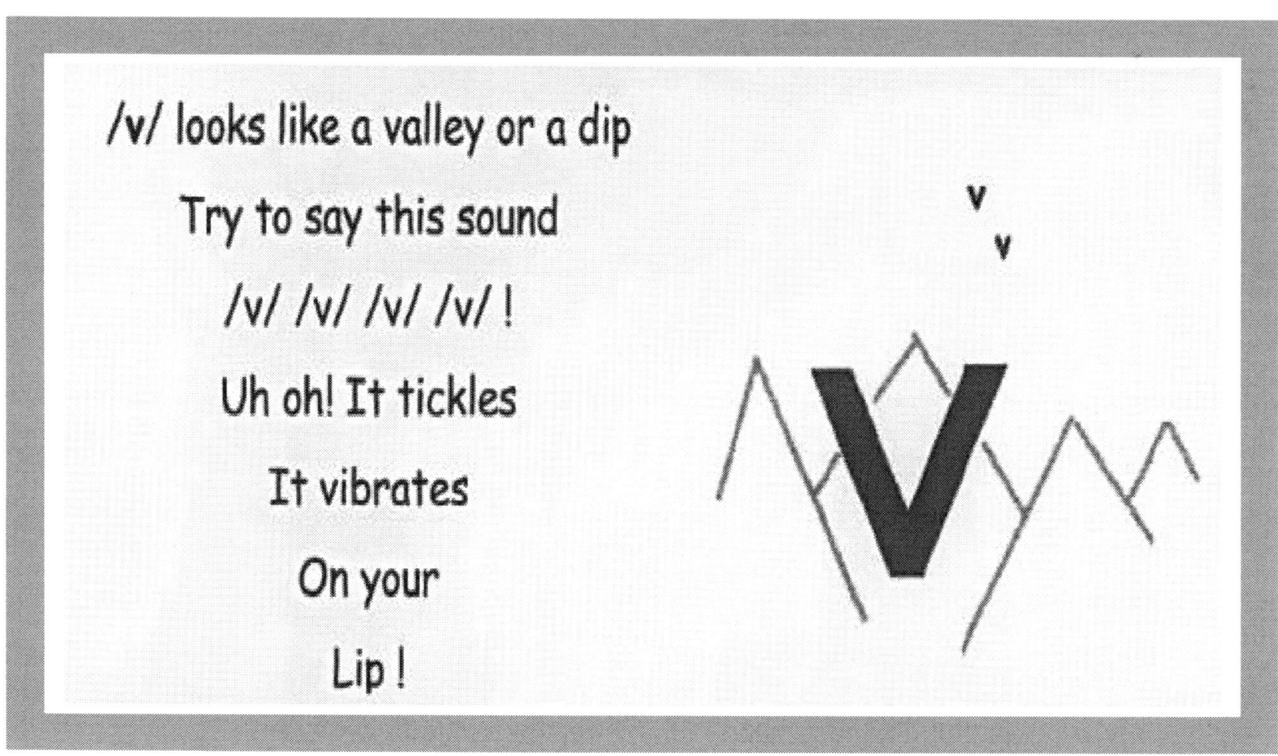

Game 4 – Valley Adventure

📖 A Wickedly Wily Word Reading Game

- Pretend you are going on an adventure together in your van.
- You start at the top of one mountain, drive down into the valley, back up the next mountain, and on to the villa (a big house).
- Take turns reading the words as you travel down into the valley and back out.
- After playing the game this way several times, see if one player can make the whole journey by himself.
- Reward with a special treat at the villa.
- If a word is read incorrectly, the other player starts from the beginning to try and complete the whole journey without error on his own.

Game 4 - Valley Adventure picture

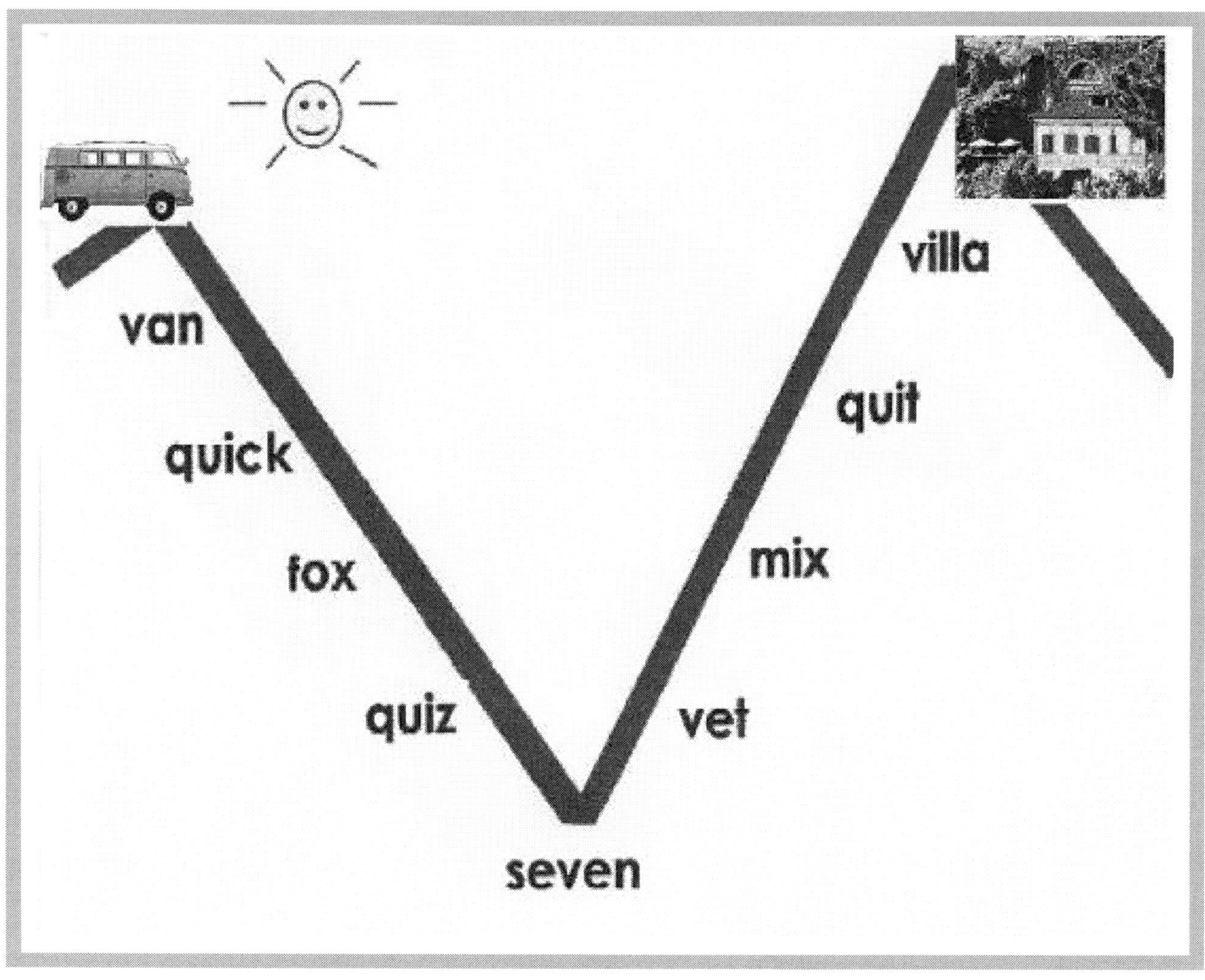

Game 5 – Shrug and Chug

☺ ***Comic Mnemonic Games***

Direct attention to the opposite page. It contains mnemonic pictures and mini-stories for the sounds /sh/ and /ch/.

Cover up the **ch** mnemonic. Now read the mini-story for the letter combination **sh,** and discuss the **sh** picture.

Ask your child the following questions:

- 'What *two* sounds are getting together to make a *new* sound?' (/s/ and /h/)
- 'What is the new sound they make?' (/sh/)
- 'Why do they make that sound?' (They are excited to be playing together but are trying to be quiet and not make too much noise.)
- 'Can you point to where you see those two letters together in the picture and the story? And can you make their sound each time?'

Uncover both mnemonic pictures. Now read the mini-story for the letter combination **ch**, and point out what is happening in the picture.

Ask the following questions:

- 'There are another two sounds getting together here. What two sounds are they?' (/c/ and /h/)
- Continue, 'When they are together they make a *new* sound too, a sound like a chugging train. What is it?' (/ch/) 'What is that sound again?' (/ch/)
- 'Can you make the sound over and over like a train chugging?' (/ch/ /ch/ /ch/)
- Ask, 'Can you point to wherever you see those two letters together in the picture, and at the same time make their sound?'

Praise your child enthusiastically throughout.

Game 5 – Shrug and Chug

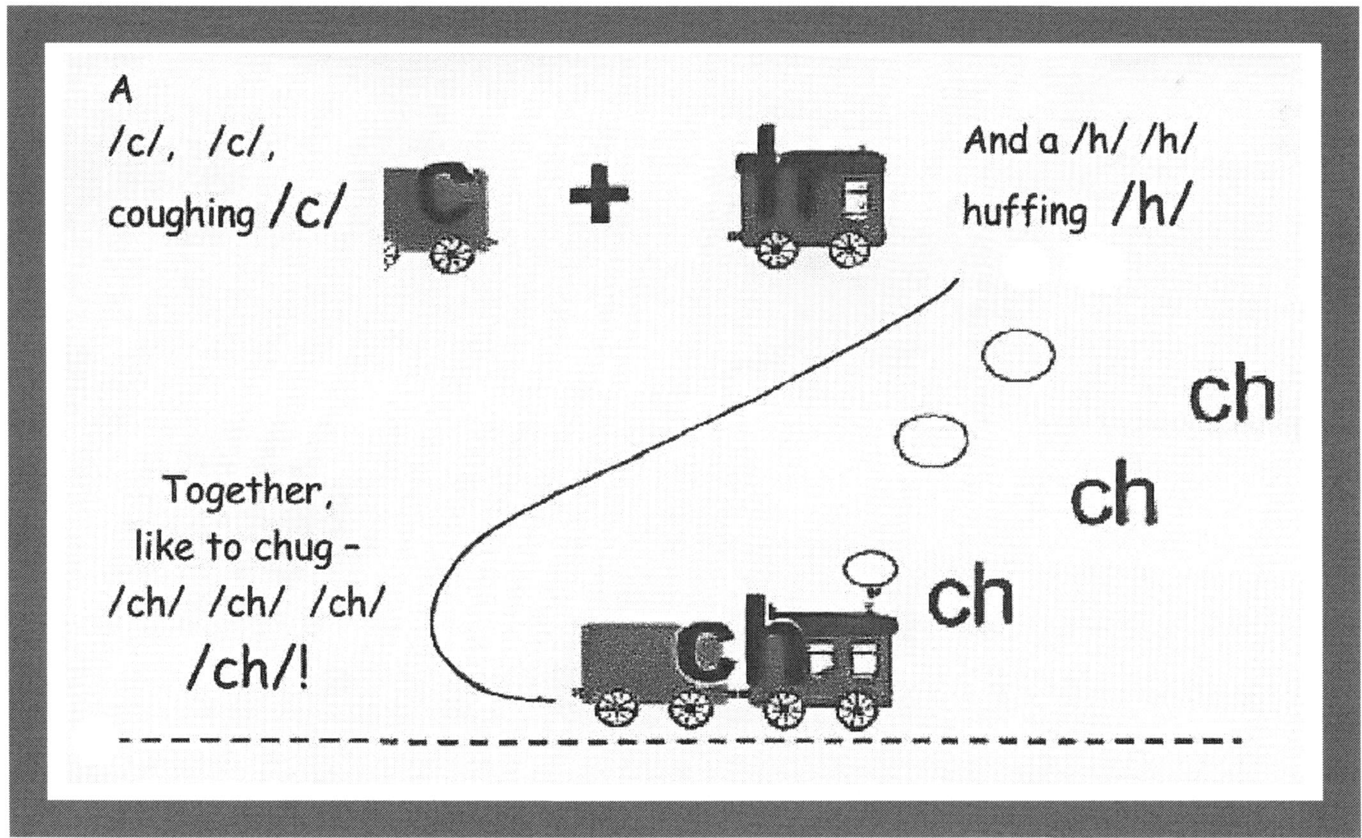

Game 6 – Fish and Chips ✋

◈ *A Mind-Bending Word Blending Game*

- Propose a trip to buy some *Fish and Chips*.

  When your child agrees, say, 'We will need some money though. So let's see if we can find some!'
- Show your child the 'money' (the first word on the list on the next page).
- Help your child to sound out the letters, and blend them together to read the word.
- If your child succeeds, he leaves a coin on the word, and can continue. Each word represents one dollar and your child will need eight dollars to buy some fish and chips. If he fails to read the word, he must start again.
- Praise your child's efforts enthusiastically. See if your child can find more 'money', sound out and read the word printed on it, and collect another dollar.
- Continue in this way until your child has collected 8 dollars.
- He can then go to the restaurant to 'buy' some fish and chips using the money he has found.
- He collects his coins, and counts out the money by reading the words, one by one, once more.
- Then he can collect a Fish and Chip treat (a snack you prepared in advance.)

Game 6- Fish and Chips 'money'

r	u	sh
c	a	sh
ch	a	t
sh	e	ll
ch	i	ck
f	i	sh
ch	i	p
sh	o	p

Game 7 – Through Thick and Thin

☺ ***A Comic Mnemonic Game***

- Show the next page to your child containing the mnemonic picture and mini-story for the soft sound /th/ as heard in the words *thick* and *thin*.
- Read the mini-story pointing out the thin letter **t**, and the thicker letter **h**.
- Explain, 'The new sound these 2 letters make when they are together is a soft windy sound, soft like a moth.' Ask, 'Can you make the sound?'
- Say, 'Place your hand in front of your mouth, and with your tongue behind your front teeth, can you feel the tiny, soft wind when you say /th/? Can you feel it when you say: *thick? thin? sloth? moth? teeth?*'
- Ask, 'Can you find the two words in the top line of text that have these two letters together?' (*thin* and *thick*)
- Ask, 'What do these two words say? Do you feel a soft wind when you say these words?' Help your child find and read other /th/ words in the text.
- Ask *yes* or *no* questions about other words: 'Can you hear the /th/ sound in the word *moth*? In the word *path? Pat? Think? Sink? Teeth? Tiny? Thank? Tank? Bath?*'
- Tell your child to repeat each word while holding his hand in front of his mouth to help him decide.

Game 8 – Thumps

A Lickety-Split Letter-Sound Game

- Show your child the words below. Ask him to find and point to the new letter combination **th** in any of the words. Each time, ask him to tell you what that part of the word *says*. Then see if he can read the whole word; then, all the words.

soft cloth   big thump   thin legs

Game 7 – Through Thick and Thin

This **thin** letter **t** and this **thick** letter **h**

Like to stick together

The new sound is sloth-y

All teeth-y and moth-y

/th/ /th/ /th/

Can you hear

How it's so soft and frothy?

Game 9 – That Tough Guy ☝

- Players take turns choosing a word card to read (p. 170). The initial strategy should be to read *all* words with the soft /th/ sound, the sound heard in the word *moth*.
- Players then ask, 'Does the word makes sense with that soft /th/ sound?'
- If a player chooses a word like *them,* she will notice it does not. When this happens, point to the *Tough Guy* picture (p. 169) and say: 'This ***/th/*** sound wants to be different; it's a tough guy! It doesn't want to make the soft /th/ sound. Instead, it says ***/th/***; make the hard ***/th/*** sound, the sound you hear at the start of the word *that*.
- Ask 'Can *you* make that tough guy sound?' Have your child make the sound while placing her hand in front of her mouth. Does she notice that there are no soft breezes coming from her mouth?
- See if your child can now read the word using the hard, 'tough guy' sound. When the word is read correctly, the player must decide which picture the word belongs with, and point to it.
- Play until all the words have been chosen. Provide lots of praise and rewards.

Note - There are more words with the soft /th/ sound, and one of these words, the word *thumb*, is a 'Tricky Word'. Simply explain that the /b/ is silent.

Game 9 – That Tough Guy ✋

Game 9 – Tough Guy word cards ✋

path	that
teeth	this
think	than
cloth	them
thump	then
tooth	thum<u>b</u>

Game 10 – At the Vet

📖 *A Wickedly Wily Word Reading Game*

- Ask your child, 'Who is the man examining the goldfish?' (A vet)
- Point to the title of this game, and help your child read it.
- Point to the word boxes and explain, 'These are the names of all the sick animals the vet had to look at today. Let's read these words and find out what animals he had to see?'
- Help your child sound out and read the words in the boxes. Keep playing until your child begins to find all of the words easy to read.
- Finally, take turns pointing to different boxes for the other player to read.

Game 11 – Matching the Vet Pictures ✋

📖 A Wickedly Wily Word Reading Game

- Players take turns to point at any one of the Game 10 word boxes (p 171). The other player must read the words and find its matching picture from this page.
- To indicate a match has been found, players can tick the words in pencil.
- When all the words have been matched with a picture, ask your child to count the *total* number of sick animals the vet had to see. (Answer = 11)

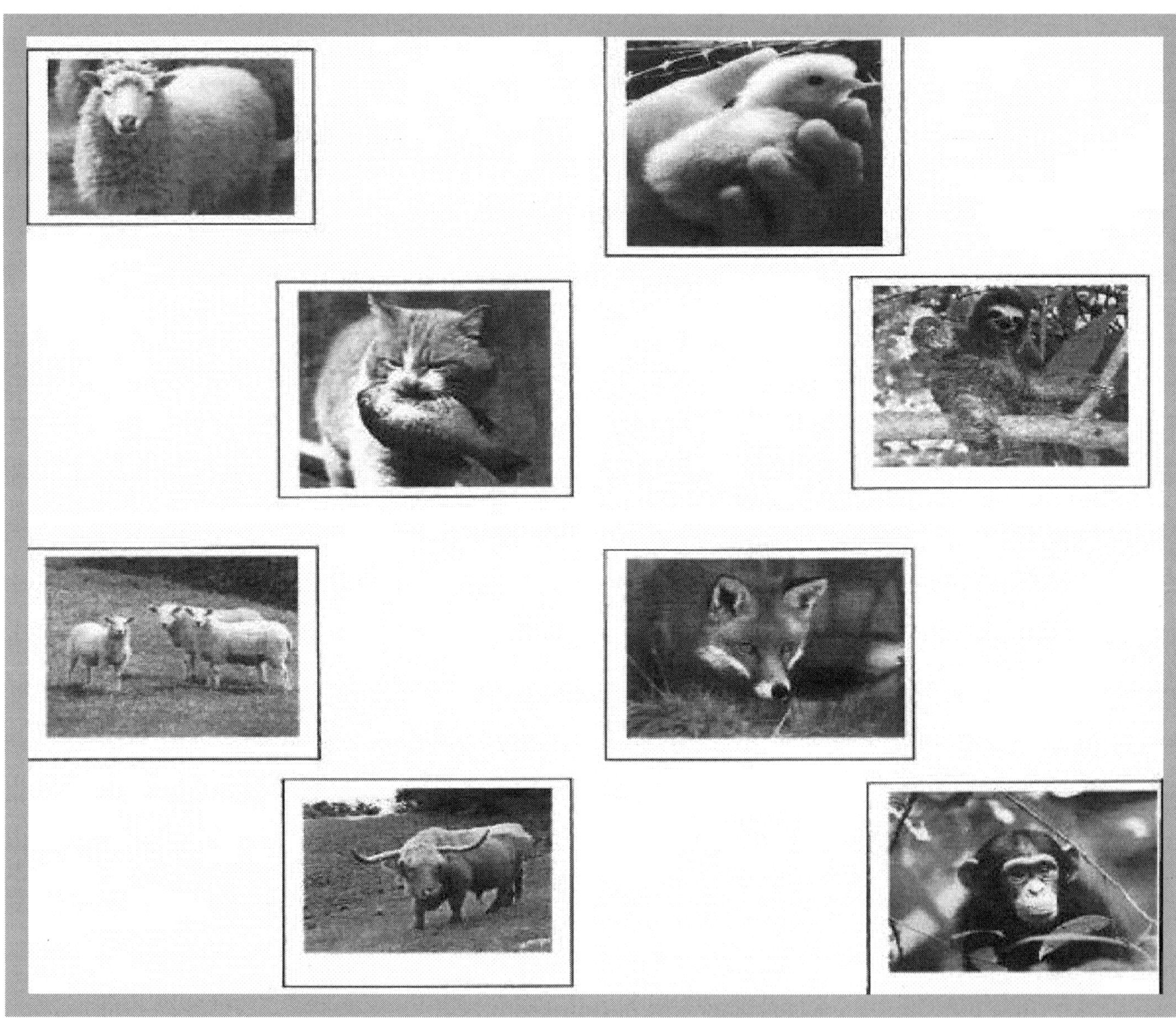

Game 12 – Shopping for Food

A Wickedly Wily Word Reading Game

- Players take turns matching words and pictures on pp 173 and174.

eggs	fish	lots of cash (ov)
shrimp	cheese (cheez)	buns
chicken	chops	milk
a box of food (ov))	ketchup	

Game 12 - Shopping for Food pictures

Game 13 – Cash and Carry (Optional)

- When all words and pictures are matched, the player with the *lots of cash* card must pay: he reads *all* the words and stacks them on top of the cash picture.
- The player with the *box of food* card, reads all the words once more, and puts the groceries (all the words) on top of the box of food picture.

Game 14 – The Tricky Game

📖 *A Wickedly Wily Word Reading Game*

There are a number of new, Tricky words in the reading booklet that follows (Game 15). But the story also includes some Tricky Words introduced previously. To review them all, play the following game first.

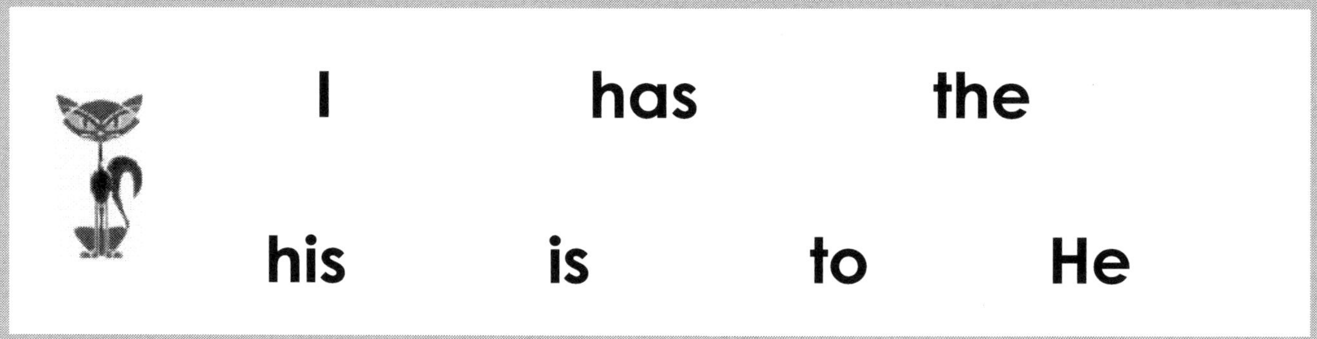

- Each sentence below has *at least one* of the tricky words in the box above hiding in it. See if your child can read the sentences, and find one of the tricky words in it from the box above that he has not previously identified.

1) Sam is a dog.

2) He is a big dog.

3) He licks the cat.

4) The cat runs to its bed.

5) I pat him.

6) I pat his back.

7) His back has spots on it.

Game 15 – Champ the Chimp

📖 *A Wickedly Wily Word Reading Game*

TITLE

- Show the next page to your child. Sound out and read the name of the story together. Ask 'Why do some of these words begin with a capital (big) letter. (Because they are words in the title, or name of the story.)
- Ask, 'What do you think this story is about?' (A chimp, or a chimpanzee)
- Ask, 'What is the chimp's name? Can you see a picture of Champ? Can you read his name?'(Say /cha/ and see if your child can finish the word.)
- Now look at the other pictures and see if your child can read the words.
- For the word *chipmunk*, show your child how to sound it out in two separate parts: *chip* and *munk*. Praise highly.

OTHER PAGES

- On all the other pages, first cover up the picture. Then, help your child read the three sentences, or the three options, praising and encouraging him.
- When he can read them all easily, uncover the picture. Ask your child to read the sentences again and find the sentence that best matches the picture.
- Show him how to check the answer key on the last page.
- What sentence number did he choose for page A, number 1, 2 or 3? Was he correct? If so, continue to read the story together.
- Remember to cover the picture each time you encounter a new page.

- Depending on your child's age, you may prefer to *take turns* reading the sentences to begin with. See how far you can go, but there is no need to complete the whole story in one session.

Champ the Chimp

Champ

van

chipmunk

1) I am Champ – a chimp.

2) I munch on green shoots.

3) This patch <u>of</u> trees has a bed.

1, 2, 3 ?

A

I will sleep on it. But soon . . .

. . . I see queer things:

1) I see a path.

2) I see a ship.

3) I see a moth.

1 , 2, 3 ?

B

I see . . .

1) a thick stick.

2) a sack in a shack.

3) a Mex¦i¦can man.

1, 2, 3 ?

C

Then I see . . .

1) a queen on a quilt.

2) a man in a rush.

3) a vet in a bath.

1, 2, 3 ?

D

I think I see . . .

1) a fish on a dish.

2) three fish with teeth.

3) fish and chips in a box.

1, 2, 3 ?

E

Next, I see . . .

1) a fox in black socks.

2) a shrimp with a limp.

3) a pinch on a cheek.

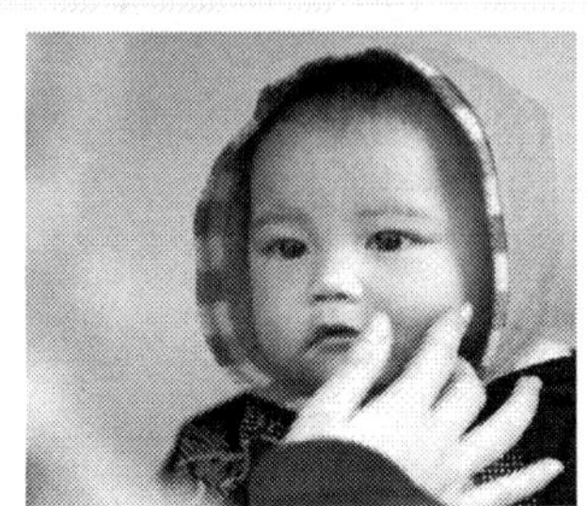

1, 2, 3 ?

F

I see . . .

1) a Dutch man with red clogs.

2) a French man with a red drink.

3) a Spanish man with a red cloth.

1, 2, 3 ?

G

I see . . .

1) a van in a ditch.

2) a chip|munk with a nut.

3) a witch mix|ing a spell.

1, 2, 3 ?

H

I see . . .

1) sev|en dots and sev|en mugs.

2) six eggs in a box.

3) three sheep in the grass.

1, 2, 3 ?

I

I sleep and sleep. I see . . .

1) a sloth on a path.

2) a shelf with dishes.

3) a catch from Max.

1, 2, 3 ?

J

I see . . .

1) a duck quacking.

2) a man fixing things.

3) a fox brushing his teeth

1, 2, 3 ?

K

I feel a crash,

a thump – a bash – and a bump!

1) I see big teeth.
2) I see a big chin.
3) I see a big cheese.

1, 2, 3 ?

L

1) I see a chest <u>so</u> big – it is vast.
2) It must <u>be</u> Dad!
3) He sends a text.
4) I run off to see Mum.

1, 2, 3 ?

M

Tricky Words in This Book

of	dishes	his	so	be
/ov/	/dish-ez/	/hiz/	/soe/	/bee/

Answers

A – 2, B – 1, C – 3, D – 2, E - 2, F – 3, G – 2,

H – 3, I – 1, J – 3, K – 2, L – 2, M – 3

Chapter 6

ai ea ie oa ue

Contents

After a time they came back home.
Toad eats a fly and crow
steals some cat food!
How happy they are.
Now it's time for a snooze.

Chapter 6

The Long Vowel Sounds

Up until now, your child has learned the *short* vowel sounds: /a/, /e/, /i/, /o/, /u/. This chapter introduces the five *long* vowel sounds and their spellings:

1) /**ai**/ (*wait*)
2) /**ea**/ (*sea*)
3) /**ie**/ (*tie*)
4) /**oa**/ (*boat*)
5) /**ue**/(*hue*)

The problem with long vowel sounds is that they have a habit of turning up in different guises. Here are just some of the ways these long vowel sounds can be spelled:

1) /ai/ - *wait, cake, play*
2) /ee/ - *sea, see* (this latter spelling, **ee** , was introduced in chapter 4)
3) /ie/ - *tie, five, I, fly, night*
4) /oa/ - *boat, nose, snow*
5) 0/ue/ - *hue, cute*

Does this seem like a mind-boggling amount of information for your child to take on board? Let me reassure you. There are four different kinds of games in this chapter: *Vowel Family* games, *Magic e* games, *Two Vowels Go Walking* games and *Exceptional* games. These games make it surprisingly easy and fun to learn about vowel spellings.

Apart from the different vowel spellings, Chapter 6 introduces the 'soft c' spelling, seen in words such as: *race*, *pencil*, and *fancy*.

1) The Vowel Family Games

Up until now, your child has learned that *one particular spelling* (one letter or a combination of letters) represents just one sound. Since this principle holds true for a large part of the English language, and *particularly for consonants*, this information is the most useful to teach at the beginning. Vowels complicate matters, however. When it comes to vowels, a number of different spellings can represent the exact *same sound* (*b**oa**t, n**o**s**e**, sn**ow***).

Your child has so far learned the most useful vowel information, the short vowel sounds: /a/ for *apple*, /e/ for *egg*, /i/ for *insect*, /o/ for *octopus*, and /u/ for *up*. The next, most frequently occurring vowel sounds are the 'long' vowel sounds. These sounds are the same as the *names* of the letters: **a**, **e**, **i**, **o**, **u**. As your child may not yet know letter names, the Vowel Family Games help your child learn them. And these games also teach your child *which* letters are vowels.

2) The Magic e Games

Your child will find his ability to recognize a vowel and remember its name very useful for reading words with a particular spelling pattern - the 'Magic e' spelling. These are words where a 2-letter vowel sound is split: they have a long vowel sound in the middle and a silent **e** on the end: *g**a**me*, *P**e**te*, *b**i**te*, *j**o**ke*, and *c**u**te*.

2) The Two Vowels Go Walking Games

The next most frequently occurring spelling pattern for a long vowel sound is where two vowels appear consecutively - in effect, the *Two Vowels Go Walking* together. These are words such as: *rain, jeans, tie, coat, hue*.

3) The Vowel Family Games

Up until now, your child has learned that *one particular spelling* (one letter or a combination of letters) represents just one sound. Since this principle holds true for a large part of the English language, and *particularly for consonants*, this information is the most useful to teach at the beginning. Vowels complicate matters, however. When it comes to vowels, a number of different spellings can represent the exact *same sound* (*b**oa**t, n**o**s**e**, sn**ow***).

Your child has so far learned the most useful vowel information, the short vowel sounds: /a/ for *apple*, /e/ for *egg*, /i/ for *insect*, /o/ for *octopus*, and /u/ for *up*. The next, most frequently occurring vowel sounds are the 'long' vowel sounds. These sounds are the same as the *names* of the letters: **a**, **e**, **i**, **o**, **u**. As your child may not yet know letter names, the Vowel Family Games help your child learn them. And these games also teach your child *which* letters are vowels.

2) The Magic e Games

Your child will find his ability to recognize a vowel and remember its name very useful for reading words with a particular spelling pattern - the 'Magic e' spelling. These are words where a 2-letter vowel sound is split: they have a long vowel sound in the middle and a silent **e** on the end: *g**a**me*, *P**e**te*, *b**i**te*, *j**o**ke*, and *c**u**te*.

4) The Two Vowels Go Walking Games

The next most frequently occurring spelling pattern for a long vowel sound is where two vowels appear consecutively - in effect, the *Two Vowels Go Walking* together. These are words such as: *rain, jeans, tie, coat, hue.*

4) The Exceptional Games

These games focus once again on words containing long vowel sounds, but their spellings do not conform to either of the two previous categories.

A Suggested 7-Day Plan

To complete the chapter 6 games with young children may require more than 20 minutes a day. However, you can proceed at a faster pace simply by playing the games for two short sessions per day. Based on two sessions a day, here is a suggested time-table:

Day	
1	Play Games 1 and 2; then play Games 3 and 4
2	Play Game 5. Then, play Game 6
3	Play Game 7; then play Games 8 and 9
4	Play Games 10 and 11. Then play Game 12 and 13a
5	Play Games 13b and c, and then play Games 13d and 14a
6	Play Game 14b and c, and then Games 14d and 15
7	Introduce the game 16 reader, *Silly Sentences*.

The Vowel Family Games

Game 1 – The Vowel Family

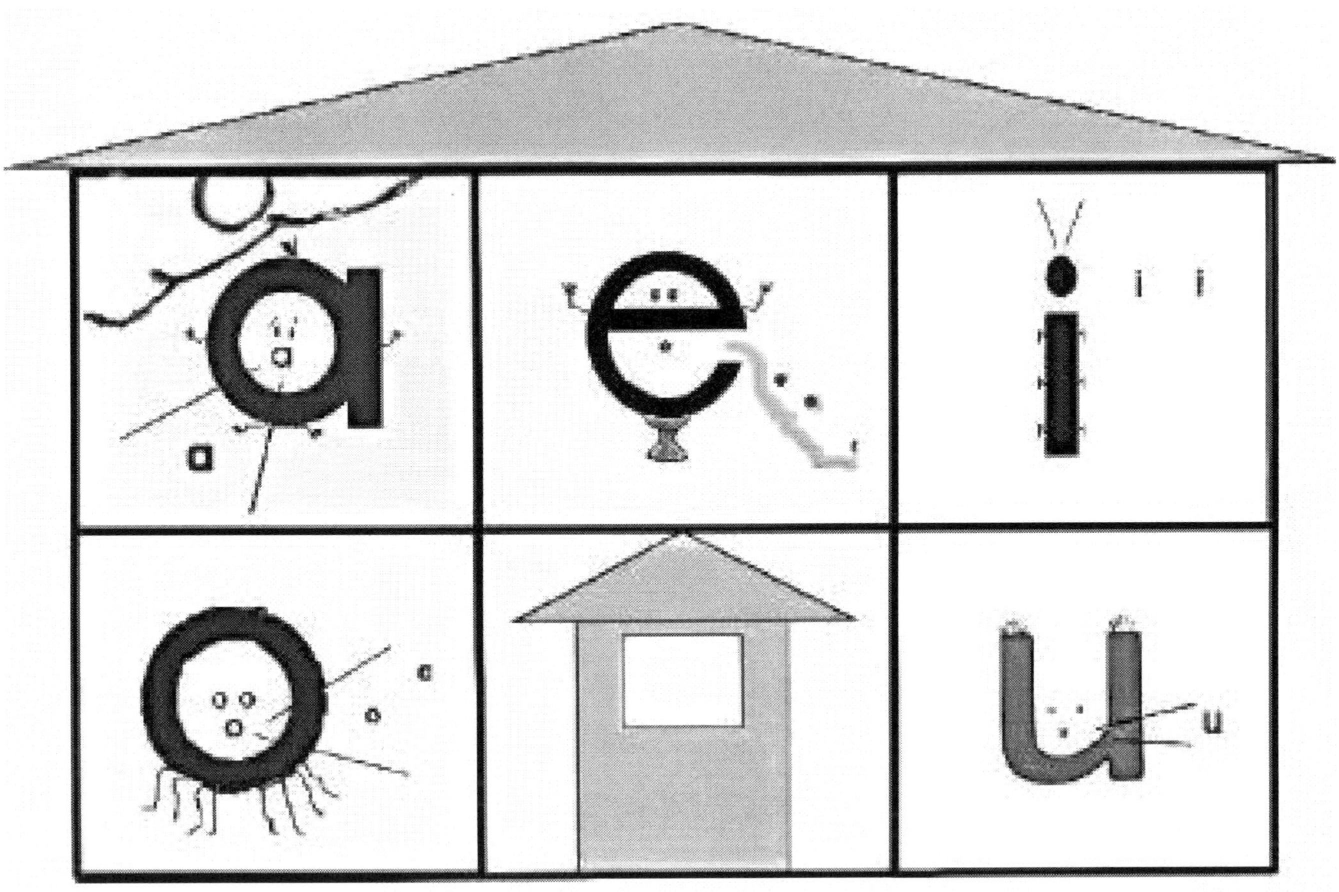

- Look at the Vowel Family picture above. Explain, 'These five letters are very special. Every word in our language has at least one of these letters in it.'
- Continue, 'They are *so* special, they even have a special name. These 5 letters are called *vowels*.'
- Check that your child remembers their *sounds* well. Point at random to letters in the house, asking 'What does this vowel *say*? And this one?'
- Then let your child point to letters and ask *you* what each one 'says'. Don't forget to make errors occasionally to ensure your child monitors you carefully.

Game 2 – Where Am I?

After playing Game 1, say, 'Clever you for remembering what the vowels *say*!'

- Now direct attention to the top half of the next page, and say, 'Here is the Vowel Family again. Now that you know what *sound* each of the vowels make, let's find out what their *names* are.'
- Point in turn to the letters, asking and explaining, 'This letter says______? But, its *name* is **ay, (ee, I, oh, you)**.'
- Repeat this exercise until your child can quickly tell you *both* the *sound* the letter makes and its *name*.
- For the letter **y,** point to it and say, 'This letter is not a real vowel. But sometimes it likes to *pretend* to be a vowel. So here he is in the Vowel House just in case he gets the chance to make a vowel sound.'
- Ask your child to find various family members in the house by *name*. Ask, 'Where is /ay/? /ee/? /I/? /oh/? /you/? And, the pretending guy, /why/?' Ask, 'Where is the vowel that *says* . . ./a/ (/e/, /i/, /o/, /u/)?' Praise enthusiastically.
- Next, *your child* can point to letters and ask *you* to find: 'The vowel that *says*___?' Or, 'The vowel whose *name* is ___?' (This is where you can act clueless from time to time to ensure your child remains on the alert.)

Game 3 – What Do You Spy?

- Recite the *Vowel Family Rhyme* on the next page together, using letter *names*, while your child points to each vowel in the Vowel Family picture.
- Repeat the rhyme, pointing to each of the vowels in the text of the rhyme.
- Recite or sing the rhyme together, until your child knows it well.

Game 2 – Where Am I?

Game 3 – What Do You Spy?

The Vowel Family Rhyme

What do you spy

With you little eye?

It's the special vowel family!

a e i o u

And don't forget

That little pretending guy ...y

Game 4 - Am I a Vowel?

- Select 12 or more lower case letter cards [Click here: 45 LETTER CARDS (pdf)].
- Make sure to include the five vowels and **y** among them.
- Put the letters in a basket or some other container.
- Take turns to choose a letter.
- Pointing out the Game 2 illustration, ask, 'Is that letter a vowel?' (Or, 'Does that letter *pretend to be* a vowel sometimes?')
- If the answer is yes, the player (you or your child) places it in the house *in its correct room*, and correctly oriented. Praise your child warmly.
- If the letter is not a vowel, the player keeps it aside for the next game.

Game 5 – Pot Luck

[If you like, before you start, fill a pot* with some little treats for your child.]

- Play this game at the end of game 4 when all the letter cards are gone.
- Each player tries to spell or 'make' a word using the letters they have put aside, along with just one vowel they choose to select from the Vowel House.
- When all the vowels in the Vowel House are gone, or neither player can make more words, the player who has made more words is the winner.
- He or she can select a lucky prize from a *pot* * containing small treats that you think your child might like.

The Magic e Games

Game 6 – Magic e

Magic e

Look at the end of a word

And maybe you will see

What is known as **Magic e**

Magic **e** has a favourite game

It makes the middle vowel in a word say its **name**

kit changes into **kite**

bit changes into **bite**

win changes into **wine**

and . . . **fin** changes into **fine**!

- Read the *Magic e* story above while pointing out various words and their features.
- Explain further, 'If there is an **e** at the end of a word, it can do a magic trick!'
- Ask, 'What is it?' (It makes the vowel in the middle of the word say its *name*!)
- Explain, 'After performing this trick, the **e** is so tired out, it makes no noise at all.'
- Point to the last 4 lines of the rhyme above, and ask your child to read the pairs of words: *kit* and *kite*, *bit* and *bite*, *win* and *wine*, and *fin* and *fine*.
- Ask your child to tell you what the vowel in the middle of each word 'says'.
- Recite the *Magic e* rhyme many times more, leaving blanks for your child to fill in.

Game 7 - The Magic Pine ☟

- Show the next page to your child. Explain, 'This is a magic pine tree! To start, we will need to read the words from the bottom.' (Point to the word *cap*).
- Take turns reading the words, praising your child enthusiastically. At the top, say, 'Well done! We've started the magic!' Now fold the page vertically to line up all the magic **e**'s at the end of the 3-letter words. (☟ extra page)
- Ask, 'What do you see at the end of each word now?'(A *Magic* **e**.)
- Say, 'We need to watch out when we read these words now, don't we? Why?' (Remind your child that a *Magic e* makes the middle vowel say its *name*.)
- Take turns once more reading the Magic e words from the bottom of the tree. For each word, ask:
  1) 'Is there a Magic **e** at the end of this word?'
  2) 'Can you point to the vowel in the middle of this word?'
  3) 'So what does this vowel say now?' (Its name)
  4) 'What *is* the name of the vowel?'
  5) 'So what does the word say?'

- Help your child sound out the word using the vowel name. Praise lavishly.

- When you reach the top of the tree, say, 'Let's see if this tree really *is* magic!'

- Help your child find a treat hiding, as if by magic, under the tree.

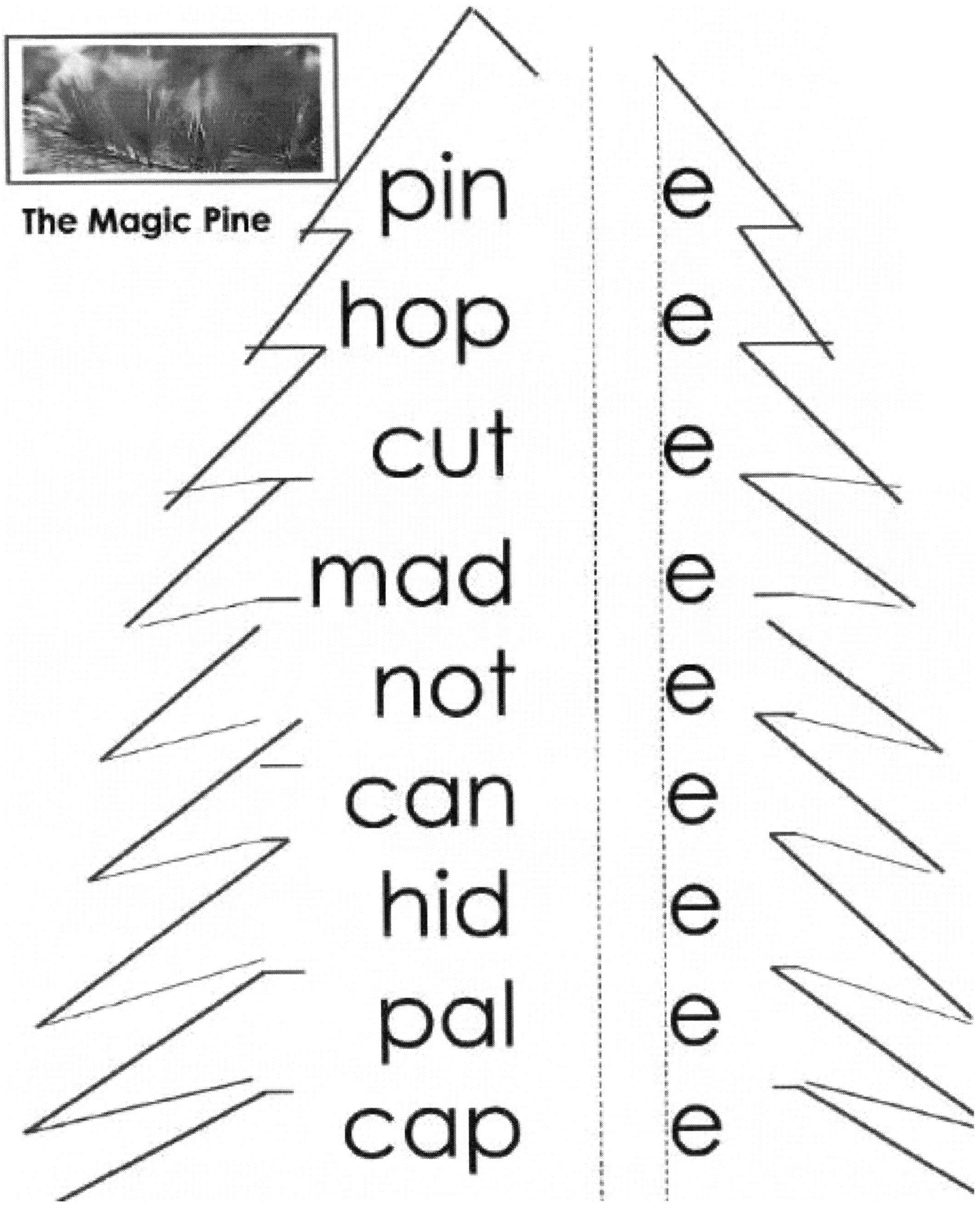
The Magic Pine
pin e
hop e
cut e
mad e
not e
can e
hid e
pal e
cap e

Game 8 – Ay, Ee, I, Oh, You? ✋

- Show your child pages pp 201- 202, listing many 'magic **e'** words.
- Ask, 'Do you see something that is the *same* about all of these words?' (See if your child notices that they all end with a *Magic e*.)
- If not using the vowel letter cards (✋), ask your child to point to one of vowels at the bottom of the page. Ask, 'What is the *name* of that vowel?
- Now ask your child to find a word on the next two pages with *that particular* long vowel sound in the middle of it.
- If he finds such a word, he now tries to read it, and if correct, he can mark the box containing that word with his own special mark (a tick, a dot, a cross) using a pencil.
- It then becomes the next player's turn to choose a vowel and name it.
- When all the words have been read and all the word boxes have been marked, it's time to count the number of words with a particular player's personal mark.
- The player who has read more words wins a prize of his choice.

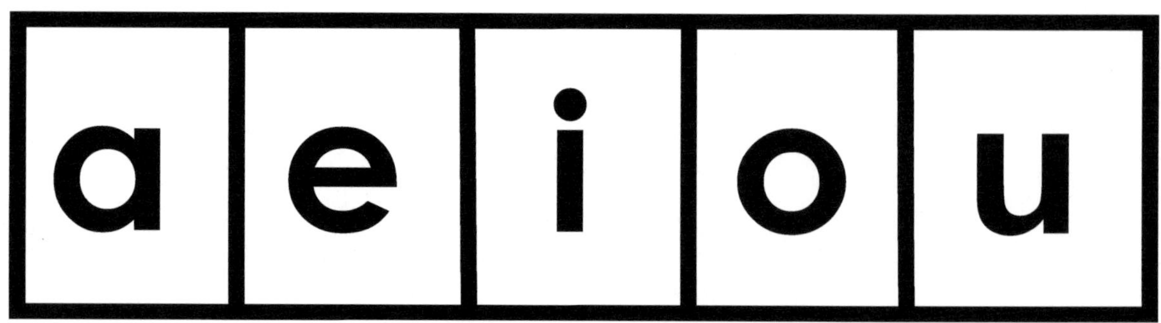

Game 8 – Magic e words

came	Eve
side	cone
cute	made
Pete	ride
joke	mute
shake	Steve

Game 8 – Magic e words (continued)

five	note
use	take
here	dive
home	late
like	cube
tape	mine

The Two-Vowels-Go-Walking Games

Game 9- When Two Vowels Go Walking

- Read the rhyme below while you point to what is happening in the picture.
- Explain, 'When you find two vowels together in the middle of a word, the first one does *all* the 'talking' and it says its own name. The second vowel doesn't have the chance to say anything!'
- Recite the rhyme together several times, pausing to ask questions, and to let your child fill in the words. Then play Game 10.

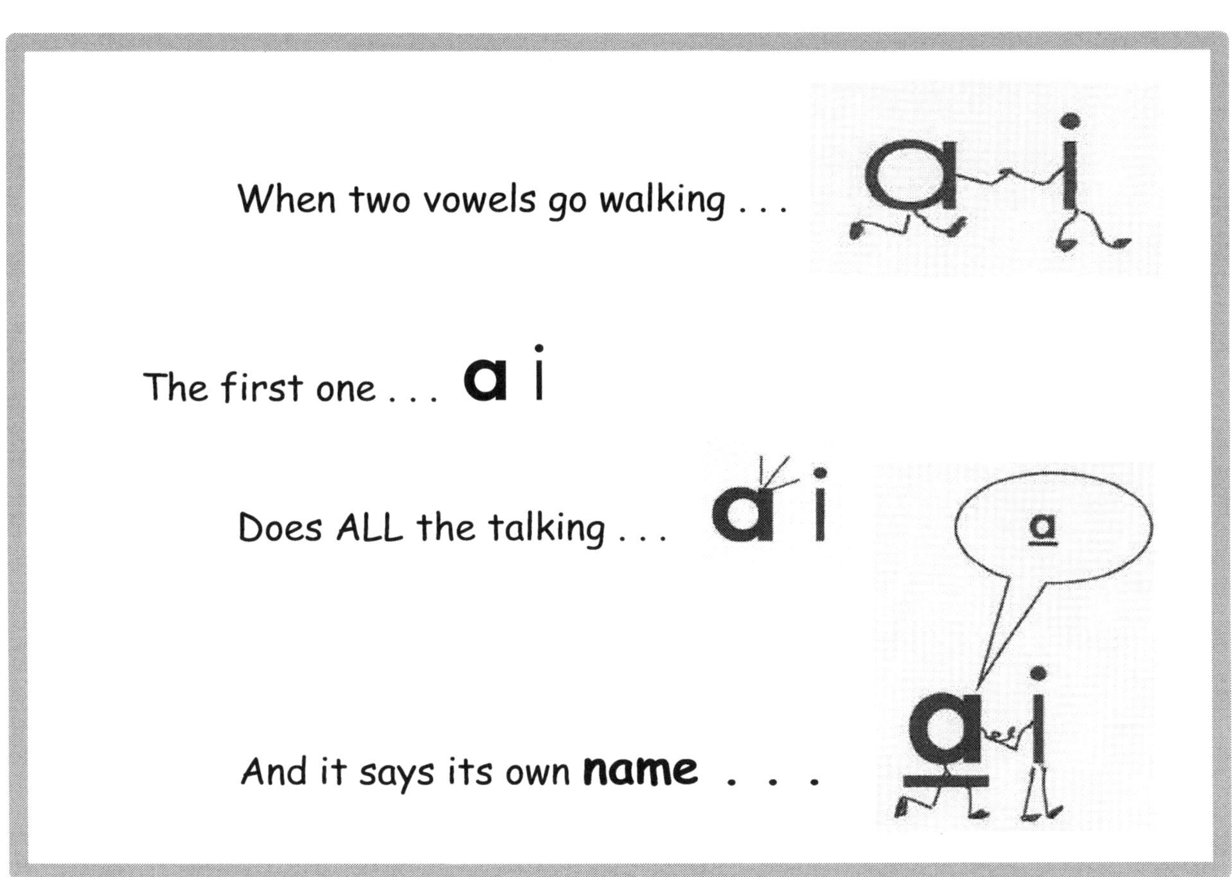

Game 10 – Walking and Talking

- Direct your child's attention to the pictures below, and say, 'Oh look! These vowels are out walking together!'
- For each pair of vowels, point to them and ask:
  1) 'Can you point to which vowel here does *all* the talking?' (Good!)
  2) 'Do you remember that vowel's *name*?' (Good for you!)
  3) 'So what do these two vowels say when they go walking together then?'
  4) 'Tell me again, what sound do they make?' (Excellent!)
- Next, take turns pointing to different vowel pairs and asking the other player to make them 'talk'. Provide plenty of enthusiastic praise.

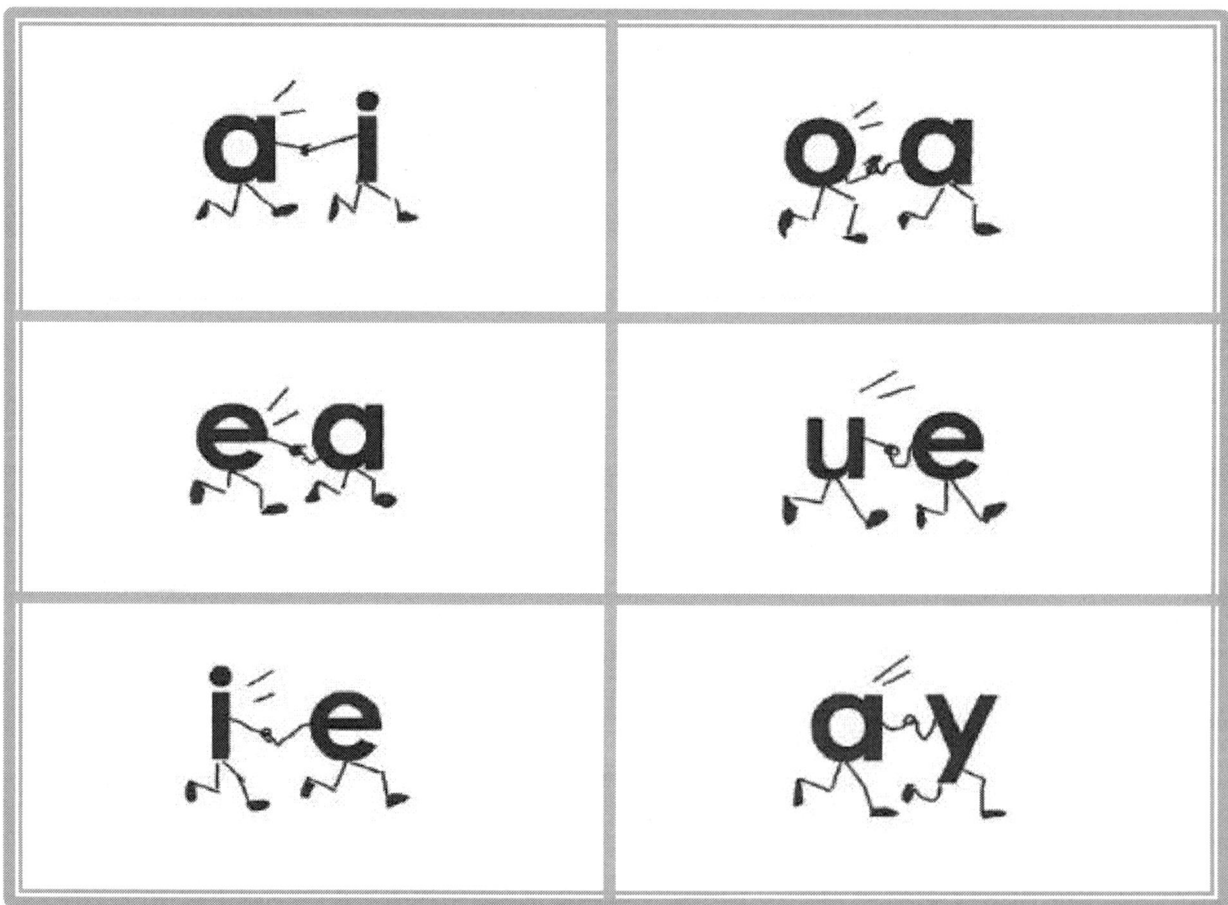

Game 11- Who's Doing All the Talking? ✋

- Turn to the next page, or obtain an extra page (✋).
- Fold the page on the two vertical dotted lines so that the first vowel is aligned right next to the second one. Say, 'Oh look! These pairs of vowels are going walking together!'
- Ask for each pair, 'Can you point to which vowel does *all* the talking?'
- When your child points to the first letter, ask 'What is that letter's *name*?'
- Ask, 'So when they go walking together, what sound do these 2 vowels make?'
- Pretend to be hard of hearing, and ask, 'What sound did you say?'
- Provide lots of praise throughout.

Game 12 – Loudmouth and Perfectly Quiet

- Now pull the page out flat, and direct attention to the list of words on the right-hand side of the page.
- Point to the first word (*mail*) and say, 'See this word? Can you point to the 2 vowels in this word? Can you point to the one that is a *loudmouth* and does *all* the talking? Can you point to the vowel that is *perfectly quiet* and says nothing?'
- Have your child repeat this pointing exercise by asking, 'Where's *Loudmouth* again? Where's *Perfectly Quiet*?' (Congratulate, 'Well done!')
- Now ask, 'So together, what sound do these 2 vowels make?'(If necessary, recite the '*When two vowels go walking….*' rhyme.)
- Then ask, 'I wonder if you can read the whole word?' Provide help as needed.
- Continue this procedure with the other words in the list. Give plenty of praise.

Games 11 and 12

a
e
i
o
e
a

i__mail
a__seal
e__pie
a__toad
y__key
y__jay

Game 13 - Let's Go Skiing! (✋ for extra p 206, and p 207 pictures)

- The previous page should be folded so the vowels are right next to each other.
- Place a tiny treat on each little 'ski' that appears after the vowel pairs (p 206).
- Say, 'Let's see if we can ski down this mountain!' (Point to its steep sides.)
- Help your child read the first word (*mail*) at the top. Ask, 'Can you find the picture that matches this word?' (see below)
- If your child makes a correct match, tell her how clever she is, and let her collect the treat on the little ski.
- Continue in this fashion until your child reaches the bottom of the mountain, has read all the words, matched all the pictures, and collected the treats.
- To play the game again, let your child pretend to zoom back up the mountain on a chair lift.
- Reload the skis with treats, and help your child 'ski' down the mountain again by reading the words and matching them to pictures as he goes.

Game 14a – 14d: Vowels on the Prowl

The following pages contain the words and pictures needed to play games 14a to 14d:

Game 14a - *The Rain in Spain* (**ai** words)

Game 14b - *The Dream Team* (**ea** words)

Game 14c - *The Goat's Boat* (**oa** words)

Game 14 d - *The Pied Piper* (**ie**, **y** and **I** words) *

- For each of the four games above (14a- 14d), begin by covering up all the *pictures* on the page with a sheet of blank paper. Then ask, 'Can you see something in all these words that is the *same*?' (Answer: All the words have 2 vowels 'going walking' in them, except for the **ie, y, I** words*.)
- Ask your child to point to the 2 vowels in every word that are 'going walking together' and tell you what they 'say' (what sound they make).
- Next, help your child sound out and read all the words, praising highly as you go.
- When your child is fluent, uncover the pictures, and take turns pointing to pictures at random to see if the other player can find its matching word.

*** Game 14d - The Pied Piper**

Explain that in this game, only *some* of the words have two vowels 'going walking' together. In the words *shy*, *dry* and *fly*, the letter **y** is *pretending* to be the vowel /i/, and it says the vowel name, **I**. (Your child already encountered the Tricky Word **I** in Chapters 4 and 5.) Explain, 'This / **I** / sound is the same sound you hear in *all* the words on this page.'

Game 14a – The Rain in Spain

rain	snail	tail
hail	nail	stain
quail	sail	train

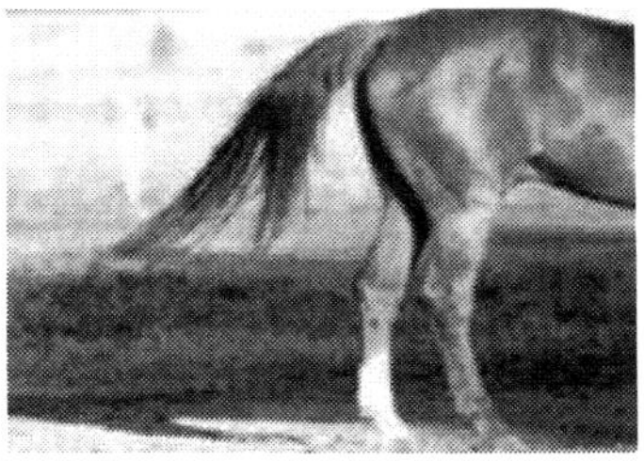		

Game 14 b – The Dream Team

leaf	eat	peas
dream	peach	sea
tea	beach	steam

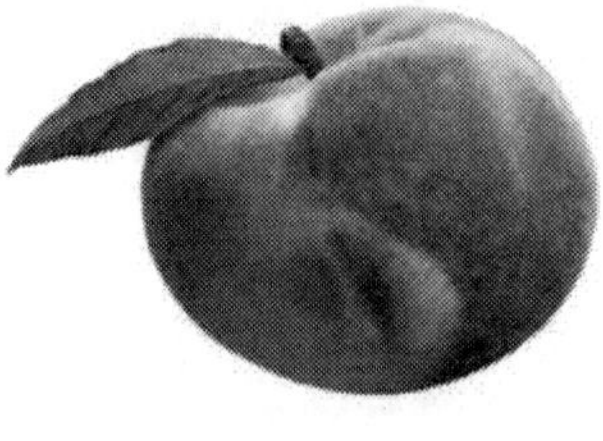

Game 14c- The Goat's Boat

coat	toad	boat
soap	goat	toast
road	cloak	coast

Game 14d – The Pied Piper

cried	tie	shy
pie	I	fried
dry	fly	lie

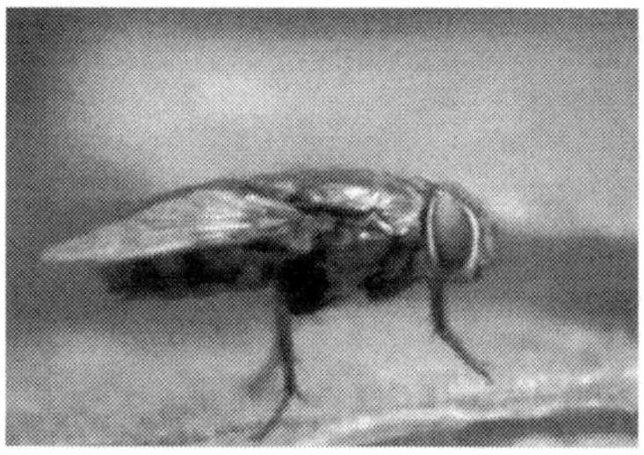

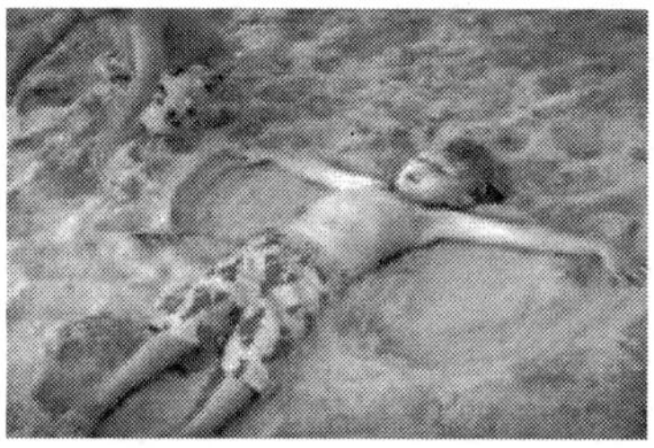

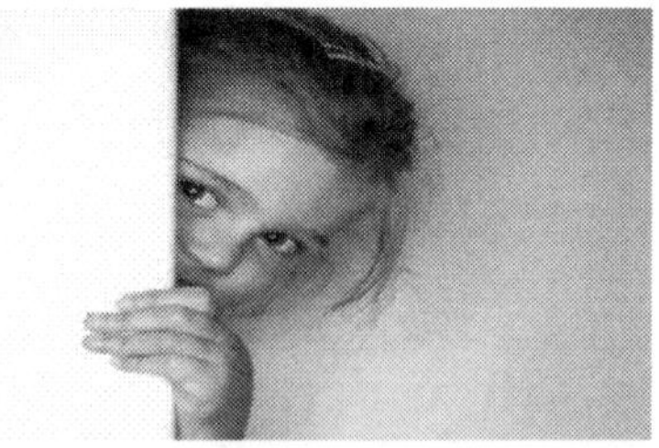

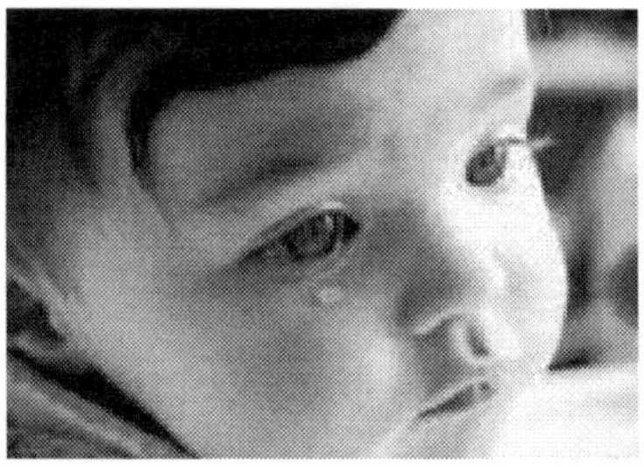

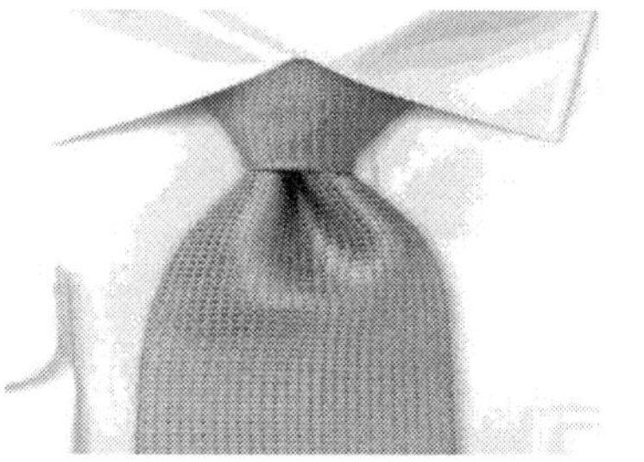

The Exceptional Games

Games 15a to 15d - Exceptionally Sorted

Some words contain the long vowel sounds **a, e, i, o**, but their spellings do not conform to the rules learned so far. Their spellings don't come into the category of *Magic e* words or *Two-Vowels-Go-Walking* words. Their spellings are exceptions to these patterns.

PART ONE -

In each of the following games (15a - d), together examine the picture boxes at the top of the page. In Game 15a, the boxes show some of the spelling patterns for the long **a** sound: **ai** as in the word *rain*, **a-e** as in the word *gate* and **ay*** as in the word *play*. (The **ay** spelling may seem like an exceptional spelling, but it actually conforms to a Two-Vowels-Go-Walking spelling pattern.)* Read the words in these boxes together and discuss what kind of spelling pattern each word has. Ask, 'Is the spelling of the word like that of:

1) a Magic **e** word?

2) a Two -Vowels-Go-Walking word?

3) an Exception–to-the-Rules word?'

PART TWO -

After initial discussion, play these three games: 1) Game 1 - Players take turns to choose a row of words for the other player to read, 2) Game 2 - Players take turns to choose a column of words for the other player to read, 3) Game 3 - Players take turns to point at words randomly, asking the other player, 'What kind of word is this? Is it a Magic e, a Two-Vowels-Go-Walking, or an Exception word?' Give rewards.

NOTE - Some exceptional spellings include: **e** (as in *me*), **y** (as in *fly*), **igh** (as in *night*), **ow** (as in *crow*), and **o** (as in *no*). Included in the long I words is the word *why*; simply explain that the **h** is silent in this word.

Game 15a – The Long A Sound

sail	snail	pain
paint	rain	wait
ate	late	game
wake	plane	cave
say	pay	stay
play	x-ray	hay

Game 15b – The Long E Sound

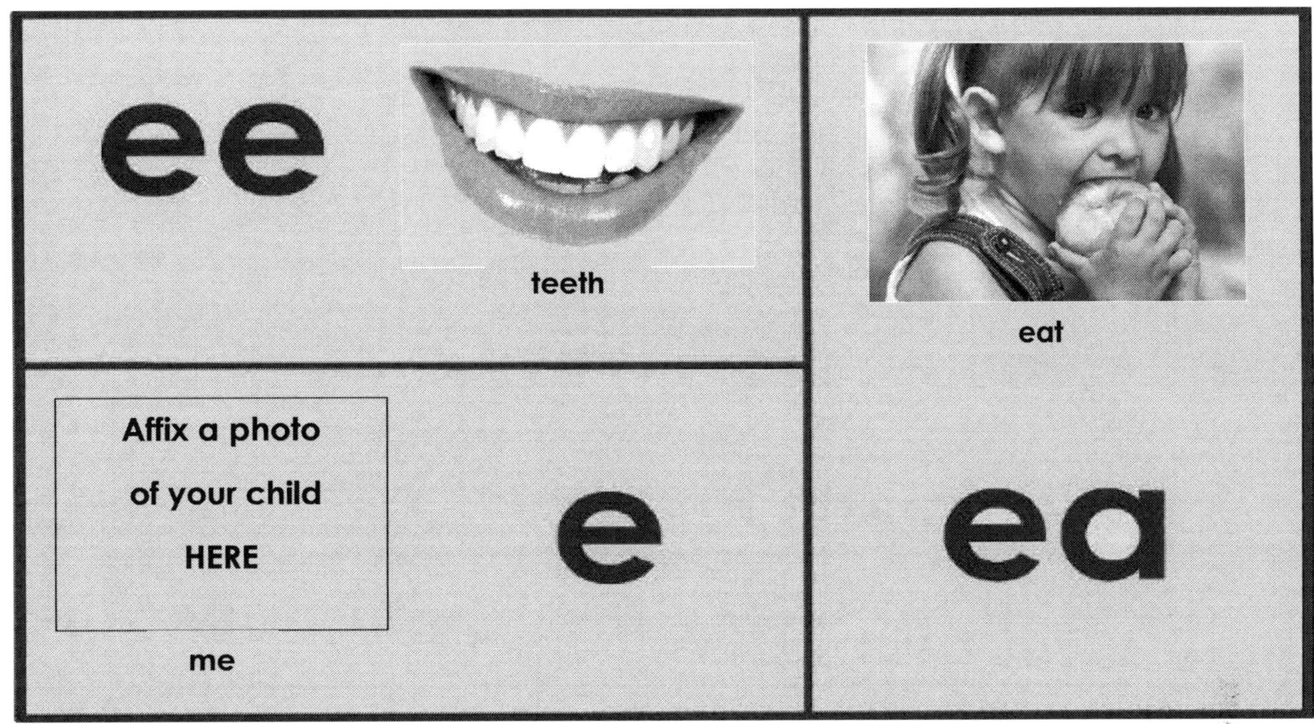

see	need	bee
feet	jeep	eat
ear	mean	heat
meal	cream	bead
leap	me	we
she	he	be

Game 15c- The Long I Sound

my	night	I
sigh	cry	fight
dry	high	fly
right	fry	sigh
try	tight	sly
thigh	why	might

Game 15d – The Long O Sound

toe	toad	crow
coat	road	moan
blow	tow	slow
hoe	show	boat
float	snow	grow
no	go	doe

Game 16 – Fancy Nancy Has a Nice Pencil

- Recite the following mini-story slowly while you point to the relevant features in the illustration below it.

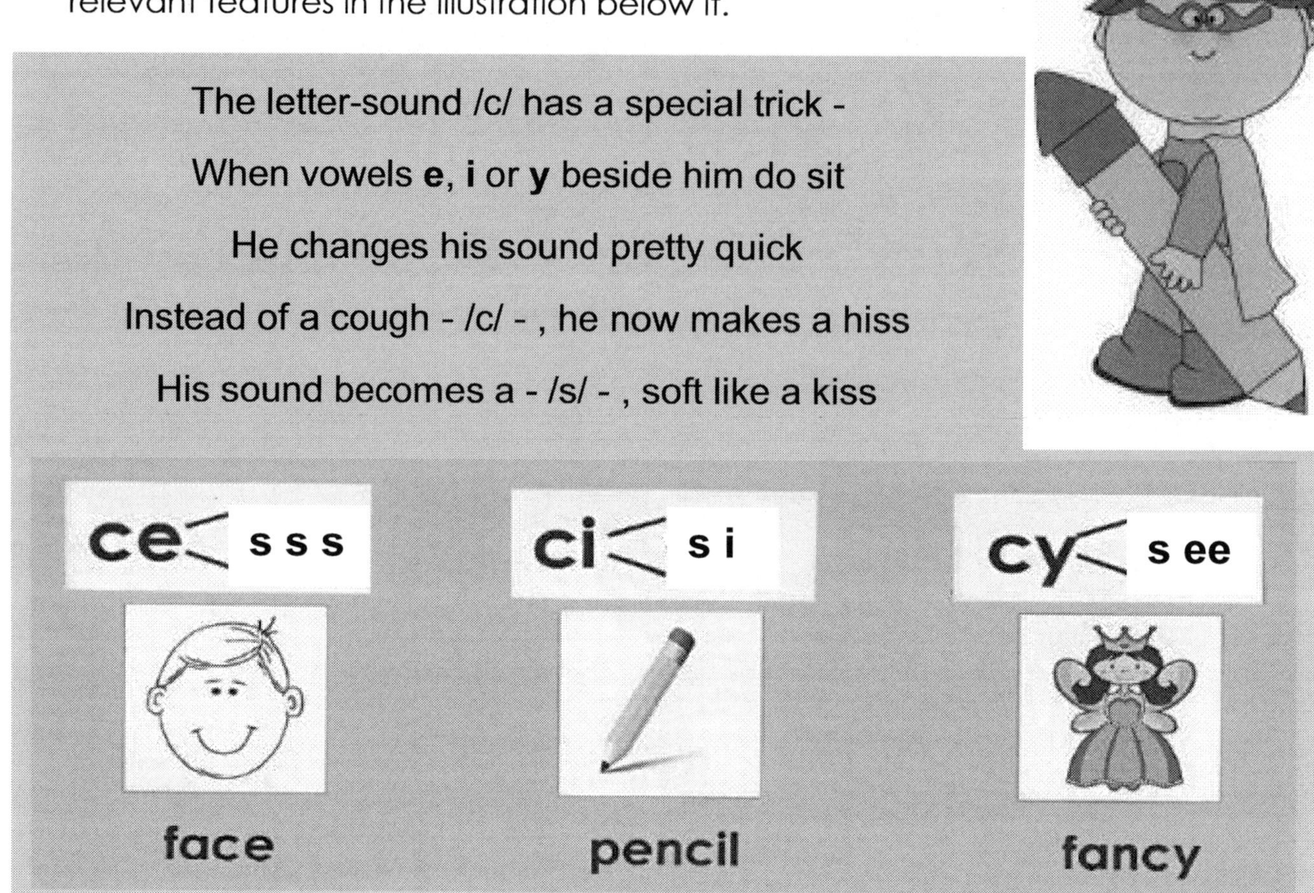

- Ask your child to point to, or underline with a pencil, the 2 letters that together make a hard /c/ sound change to a soft /s/ in the following words:

ice	nice	mice	race	twice	place
icy	excite	fancy	pencil	spicy	prince

- Take turns reading the words. Provide help and encouragement as needed.
- Ask, 'Can you read the name of this game?' Give lots of PRAISE.

Game 17- Silly Sentences

There are two versions of this game: Super *Silly Sentences* (requiring extra materials) and *Super Silly Faces* (where the book can be used as it is.

Super Silly Sentences:

[Click on this link to obtain the sentence beginnings and endings; find Game 17, p 35; BOOK SUPPLEMENT FOR OPTIONAL USE (pdf). Cut on dotted lines to make a collection of sentence beginnings and sentence endings. Arrange them in two piles, the beginnings on the left, and the endings, on the right.

- Players should sit side by side with the two piles of paper slips in front of them.
- Players now take turns choosing one slip from each pile.
- Next, players must line up their two paper slips to make a complete sentence.
- Players then take turns to read their sentence. Once they are able to read their sentence fluently, they leave it in place in front of them.
- The player who is the first to make, and read, more silly sentences wins a special chance to choose a reward from a container. This container should contain mostly silly, miscellaneous items, and a few desired items.

Super Silly Faces:

If you prefer to use the sentence beginnings and endings page as it is, without having to print and cut, ensure that you have a bag or a basket containing paper slips numbered from 1 to 9. Then play the game as follows:

- Players choose a numbered slip and read the 'sentence beginning' on the following page with that number.
- When all the numbered slips have been chosen, players take turns reading their 'sentence beginnings' and choose one of the 'endings' on the following page to combine with it. If they are able to make and read a whole sentence, they receive a token (a button, a bead, a coin).
- The player with more tokens at the end of the game can demand that the other player make silly faces. This must continue until the player observing the faces shows that he is amused via a tell-tale sign – a laugh, a smile, a giggle or a smirk.

- Optional Flip Reader – Using the picture box on the previous page as a front cover and the box below as a back cover, make a booklet with lined pages. Staple across the top. Cut the pages inside in half vertically up to the staple line. Then print sentence beginnings and endings on the page halves for your child to flip and create silly sentences to read.

SENTENCE BEGINNINGS	SENTENCE ENDINGS
1. That nice striped cat smiles and	tells the snowman a joke.
2. That mean witch eats toads and	rides on a crocodile.
3. The moose makes toast and	pokes the mailman
4. Kate licks an ice cream cone and	hides in a cave.
5. Batman wakes up at night and	then swims in the waves.
6. Dave has a fright and	sits on a big juicy grape.
7. An ape by the name of Nate	bites the stove.
8. Bruce paints his face green and	drives to the lake.
9. A goose steals my pillow and	flies high up in the sky.

Chapter 7

ar or er ou oi oo

Contents

Chapter 7

The Final Six Sounds

Welcome to the final chapter of this book. You will have now introduced your child to 36 out of the 42 sounds heard in the English language. This final chapter introduces the remaining 6 sounds:

1) /ar/ (as in the word *car*),
2) /or/ (as in the word *snore)*,
3) /er/ (as in the word *tiger*),
4) /oi/ (as in the word *oink*),
5) /ou/ (as in the word *mouse*), and
6) /oo/ (as in the word *look*).

After playing these final Chapter 7 games, your child will be in an excellent position to tackle the majority of words found in nearly all printed materials. Most important, your dedication in teaching your child to read at an early stage will have changed the course of his or her life forever! You will have dramatically increased the chance for extraordinary success in all facets of your child's life.

Spelling alternatives for the new sounds

The six new sounds all involve vowel sounds, and as explained in chapter 6, vowel sounds often turn up spelled in different ways. So, while there are six new sounds, there are at least ten different ways in which these sounds are commonly spelled. Organizing the spellings into the following four groups helps to make sense of them.

1) R-Controlled Vowel Sounds

- The sound /ar/ is spelled **ar** (*car*)
- The sound /or/ is spelled **or** (*snore)*
- The sound /er/ can be spelled **er** (*tiger*), **ur** (*purr*), or **ir** (*whirr*)

2) Vowel Combination Sounds

- The sound /ou/ can be spelled **ou** *(mouse)*or **ow** (*brown*)
- The sound /oi/ can be spelled **oi** *(oink)* or **oy** (*boy*)

3) Old and New Sounds and Spellings

- The new sound /**oo**/ (as in the word *look*) is spelled **oo**, a spelling introduced in Chapter 4 for a different sound (/oo/ as in the word *moose)*.
- The sound /ee/, can be spelled **ee** (as introduced in Chapter 4), or with a **y** (*funny*).

4) Country-Related Alternate Sounds and Spellings

- The sound /o/ is spelled **aw** (*saw*) in the USA and Canada.
- The sound /or/ is spelled **aw** (*saw*) in the UK, Australia and NZ.

A Suggested 7-Day Plan

Chapter 7 contains a fair amount of new information to introduce to your child. To complete these games in one week, play each day for one longer session of 30+ minutes each day, or play games in two separate sessions a day, each about 20 minutes. If your child is young, however, you may prefer to take longer to complete the games contained in this chapter. There is no pressure. Feel free to take up to two weeks to play the chapter 7 games. Keep in mind that the top priority is to enjoy yourselves.

A Suggested 7-Day Plan

Day

1 Play Games 1 and 2, introducing the sounds /ar/ and /or/. Then play Game 3 to introduce the /er/ sound.

2 Play Game 4 to practise reading words containing different spellings for the /er/ sound. Play Game 5, explaining the three sounds the letter **y** can make.

3 Play Game 6 to review the new sounds learned so far. Play Games 7 and 8 which explain the two sounds made by the letters oo (as in the words *moose* and *book*).

4 Play Game 9 and 10 to introduce the new sound /oi/. Then play Game 11, introducing the new sound /ou/.

5 Play Game 12, explaining an alternative spelling for the sounds /o/ and /or/. Play Game13, introducing the first reader in a series of three readers - The *Crow and the Toad.*

6 Play Game 13 again. Then read the second reader, *The Cat and the Mouse.*

7 Read the second reader once more. Then, read the third reader, the *Dog and the Farmer*. Encourage your child to read all three readers, which are linked in one story, until he or she is fluent.

R-Controlled Vowel Sounds

Game 1 - /ar/ and /or/ Like to Roar

- Ask, 'Do you remember that /r/ makes the roaring noise /errr/ like a /rocket?'
- Ask, 'Can you make that roaring sound?' (Well done!)
- Tell your child, 'If /r/ (er) has a vowel in front of it, it can make even *more* noise!'
- Point below and say, 'Look what happens when an /a/ gets together with an /r/: an /a/ with an /r/ makes the noisy sound **/ar/,** like the engine of a fancy. . . . .

- Ask, 'Can you point to the 2 letters in the word *car* that make the /ar/ sound?' Point to the letters **ar** at the back of the car and ask, 'And, more loudly?'
- Say, 'Look at the picture below. What happens when an /o/ gets together with a noisy /r/?'
- 'An /o/ with an /r/ makes the sound /or/, like someone who has a loud . . . . .

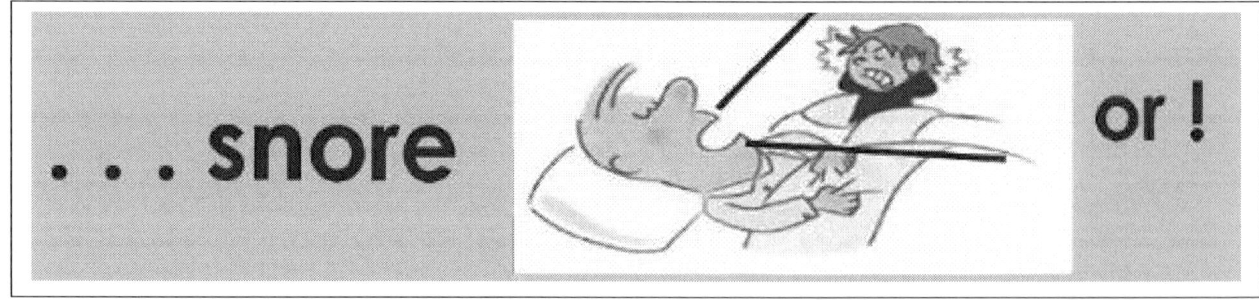

- Ask, 'Can you point to the two letters in the word *snore* that say - /or/?'
- Point to the letters **or** and ask, 'Can you make this sound? And, more loudly?' (Well done!)

Game 2 – Noisy Words

- Say, 'Let's make some more loud noises together now.'
- Point to the box below and explain, 'Here are some words where noisy /r/ (pronounce the sound /er/) has attached itself to some vowels, so that he can make even more noise!'
- Step 1) Take turns reading, one by one, just the *underlined parts* in the words below. Provide lots of exuberant praise.
- Step 2) Take turns to read the underlined parts in *all three lines* of words. (When it is your turn to do this, make occasional errors to keep your child on the alert.)
- Step 3) Take turns reading the words, helping your child as needed.
- Step 4) The player who can read *all three lines* of the words by himself without error receives a star-shaped reward (sticker, cookie, cracker, badge …)

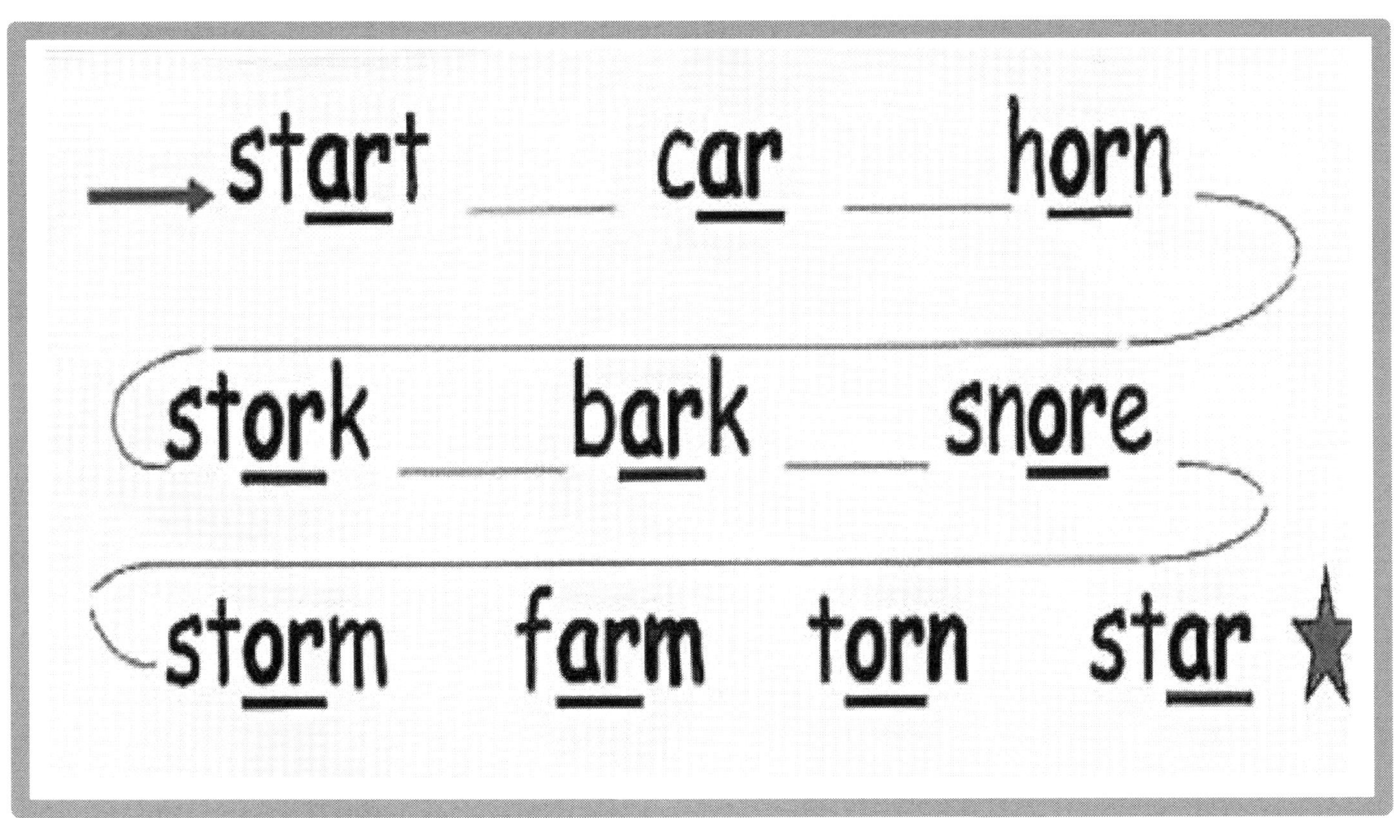

Game 3 – The /er/ Family

- Point to the underlined parts in the words above. Each time say, 'This says /er/.' Ask, 'Can you make that sound?' PRAISE.
- Point to the underlined parts in each word once again, and ask, 'All these words have a noisy /r/ sound in them. But in every word, what kind of special letter do you see along with every /r/ sound?' (a vowel)
- Ask, 'Can you point to the part in each word that says /r/ (er)?'
- In random order, point to the parts of each word underlined and ask, 'What does this part say again?'
- Help your child read the three words while you explain their oddities:
- In the words *whirr* and *purr*, the two **r**'s make just one sound.
- In the word *tiger*, the /i/ says its *name*, **I.**
- In the word *whirr*, the /w/ and /h/ make just *one* sound together, /w/.
- Point at random to the 3 words and help your child to read them several times.
- Praise highly: 'You are so clever! Are you clever enough to read this word, I wonder?' ⟶ **clever**

Game 4 – First Blind Tiger to Thirteen

- One player is blindfolded and becomes a . . . 'Blind Tiger'.
- Then, with guidance from the other player, he points at random to one of the words below.
- With his finger glued to the page, the blindfold is removed and he tries to read the word that is nearest to the spot he selected.
- If successful, he wins a token (button, coin, bead . . .) and his turn ends.
- As soon as one player has collected thirteen tokens, he wins a super prize.

fir	stir	ever
her	jerk	turn
hurt	surf	girl
bird	shirt	letter
sister	softer	purse
burn	curl	chirp

A New Spelling for the Sound /ee/

Game 5 – The Funny Guy y

1) Show this page to your child and say, 'The letter **y** '(say its letter name) 'usually says /y/' (say its sound):

- Ask 'What is the letter **y** saying here?'
- Ask, 'What does the word say?'
- Congratulate, 'Good for you!'
- Say, 'But this letter doesn't always say /y/ like it does in the word *yes*.'

2) Sometimes, **y** likes to say - /ie/ (I):

- Explain, '**Y** is quite a funny guy. Do you remember that sometimes **y** likes to *pretend* to be a vowel?'
- Remind your child of the Vowel Family Rhyme: 'What do you spy with your little eye? It's the special Vowel Family – **a, e, i, o ,u**, and don't forget that little pretending guy . . . **y.**'
- Direct attention to the word below and say, 'In this word, the letter **y** is *pretending* to be the vowel /i/, but it says the *name* of that vowel, - I.'
- Ask, 'So what does the word say?' (/slie/

Review by saying, 'So the letter **y** can say /y/ like it does in the word *yes*, but it can also pretend to be the vowel /i/ and say its *name* - I, in a word like *sly*.

3) At the end of other words, though, **y** has *another* trick. It likes to say - /ee/.Point to the word below and ask, 'What is happening here? What is that Funny Guy **Y** saying in this word?' (/ee/)

funny ee

- Ask, 'Can you read the word?' Provide help as needed. Praise highly and explain, 'The Funny Guy **Y** at the end of this word is *pretending* to be the vowel /e/. But, the sound he makes is the *name* of that vowel - /ee/.' Ask, 'So what does this word say again?'

- Point to the word *Mummy* and say, 'This word has that Funny Guy **Y** at the end of it too! Maybe you can read this word?' Congratulate enthusiastically.

Mummy

- Now have your child read the different **y** words on these two pages (*yes, sly, funny, Mummy, yummy*).

- You might then wish to reward your child with something that is truly . . . . . .

yummy!

Game 6 - Birthday Party

Before you start this game, put some real party favours (party hats, balloons, horns, whistles or other treats) in a basket in a hidden location.

Step 1 – Pretend that you are getting ready to go to a birthday party and first need to wrap up some birthday presents.

- On the next page are a list of phrases; one can pretend these are pieces of wrapping paper.
- Players take turns choosing wrapping paper and reading the words on it.
- On their next turn, they look for the picture of the present to be wrapped.
- If correct, the player draws a line in pencil to match the paper to the picture.
- When all the phrases (wrapping paper) and pictures (gifts) have been matched, players move to different location (the birthday party venue).

Step 2 - At the party location, players pretend to exchange gifts and unwrap them.

- Players take turns pointing to pictures (gifts) that they did *not* wrap up.
- If they can find and read the matching wrapping paper phrase, they are awarded one of the birthday party favours.
- And each time this happens, all the players celebrate by shouting 'Happy Birthday!'

'Wrapping Paper' (word slips)	'Presents' (pictures)
a furry squirrel	
a funny birthday cake	
a nifty digger	
party horns	
a sparkly star	
a sharp fork	
a yummy tart	
a faster car	
a silly card	

A New Sound **oo** as in Look

Game 7 – Look! A Moose!

- Ask, 'Both words in the box above have something the *same* about them. Can you see what it is?' (Both words have two **o**'s.)
- Point to the word *moose* /moos/and help your child sound it out and read it. Praise. Then point to the word *look* /look/and ask your child to read that word.
- If your child reads the word *look* with the same /oo/ sound heard in the word *moose*, ask, 'Do you think there is something strange about that? Is there such a word? Can you guess what the word really is? Do you think it says *look*?'
- Point to the vowel combination **oo** in each of the two words above, and ask what different sound the two letters make in each word. (/oo/ and /oo/)
- Ask your child to repeat the two different sounds many times - /oo/ and /oo/.
- Ask your child to read the name of the game several times.
- Make sure to shower plenty of praise throughout.

Game 8 – A Moose on the Loose

- Remind your child, 'When two **o**'s get together they don't always say /oo/ as they do in the word *moose*.'
- Sometimes when two letter **o**'s are together, they say /**oo**/ like the sound you hear in the words *look*, *cook*, and *book*.
- Explain and point, 'Here is a story with both kinds of words in it.'
- Warn your child, 'But watch out! You will have to read the story very carefully before you can decide what kind of /oo/ sound these words have in them.'
- Ask your child to read the two words of encouragement below before starting:

Good luck!

A moose stood in the

woods under the moon.

It is quite a cool night.

But, look! The moose is lucky.

He has a good woollen coat.

Vowel Combination Sounds /oi/ and /ou/

Game 9 – The Pointing Game

- Explain, 'This game is all about a *new* sound, the sound /oi/. It's the sound you hear in the word *oink.*' (Point above to the letters **oi** in the middle box.) 'It's also the sound you can hear in the word *boy.*' (Point above to the letters **oy**).
- Ask, 'Can *you* make that /oi/ sound? And, again? And, more loudly?' (Yes you can! Well done!)
- Ask, 'Can you point to two letters that say /oi/?' (Good!) 'And, can you point to *another 2 different letters* that say /oi/ too?' (Well done!)
- Ask, 'Can you point to what the pig is saying? And, can you tell me what the word is?' (Excellent!)
- Ask 'Can you point to the two letters in the word *oink* that say /oi/? (Good!)
- Ask, 'Underneath the picture of the boy, there is a word. Can you read it?' (Boy, oh boy! Good for you!)
- Ask, 'Can you point to the 2 letters in the word *boy* that say /oi/?'
- Ask, 'Can you point to the name of the game?' (Yes, you found it!)
- Ask, 'What *is* the name of the game? Can you read it?' (You are so clever!)Then say, 'I wonder if you can read the name of the next game?' (Well done!)

Game 10 - A Toy Story

- Ask your child to point to all the vowel combinations that say /oy/ contained in the words in the box below.
- Now help your child follow the arrows and read all the /oi/ words.
- Next, take turns to ask the other player to find a particular word and point to it.
- Whenever a player points to the word toys, the other player has a chance to win a reward.
- First, however, he must think of a sentence that has at least one word with the sound /oi/ in it.

→ point → boy → oil

join → boil → coin → soil

coin → spoil → moist

voice → oyster → toys →

Game 11 – Brown Mouse

ow / ou

brown mouse

- Show this page to your child.
- Explain, 'This game is all about another new sound, the sound /ou/.' Ask your child to say the sound repeatedly in a tiny, *brown mouse* voice.
- Point, in turn, to **ow** and **ou** in the box above, and say, 'This says /ou/, and this says /ou/ too! What does this word part say again? And this one?' (Good!)
- Ask, 'In this word *brown*' (point), 'can you point to the part that says /ou/?'
- Ask, 'In this word mouse' (point), 'can you point to the part that says /ou/?'
- Ask, 'In all the words below, can you point to the 2-letter part that says /ou/?'
- Ask, 'Can you read each word below and find its matching picture?' PRAISE.

Alternate Sounds and Spellings

Game 12 – The Fawn on the Lawn

The spelling **aw** is an alternative spelling for the sound /o/(in the USA) and /or/ (in the UK). Using your normal pronunciation, help your child read the sentences below. Then, take turns reading the sentences again. See who can find the matching picture first. [Explain that in the word *large*, the letters **ge** say/j/ (in sentence number 6)].

1) A brown fawn stood on the lawn.

2) She uncurls and yawns after a nap.

3) Can you hear the caw of the crow?

4) 'Ouch!' This crab has sharp claws!'

5) The girl and boy saw fresh prawns.

6) Look! I spy a large strawberry!

Review Games

Game 13 – A Farm Mys ter y (/miss- ter- ee/)

- The following pages contain three small reading booklets:
    1) *The Crow and the Toad*
    2) *The Cat and the Mouse*
    3) *The Dog and the Farmer*

- For each reader, help your child sound out and read the name of the story.
- To begin with, you can take turns reading sentences.
- Later, encourage your child to read whole pages and the whole book all by himself.
- The key to motivating your child is to let him know how impressed and proud you are with his reading.
- Tell your child often just how very clever he is.
- From time to time, ask questions about the content and the pictures as your child is reading to check that he understands what the story is about.
- The Tricky Words are underlined, and are listed on the back cover of each booklet.
- Your child can check to see if a difficult-to-sound-out word is listed there, and see how the word should be pronounced if it were spelled according to normal spelling rules.

The Crow

and the Toad

The Crow and the Toad

The crow is up high in the tree.

She is looking down on the farmyard.

'I see you', she shouts at the toad.

The toad is down by the pond.

1

'I see you, too' <u>says</u> the toad.

Down <u>comes</u> the crow.

She lets toad leap on her back.

Off <u>they</u> go,

way up in the sky.

2

After a time they <u>come</u> back home.

Toad eats a fly.

Crow steals <u>some</u> cat food.

How happy they <u>are</u>.

Now it's time for a snooze.

3

The Crow and the Toad

Page:	1	2	3
	She	**says**	**come**
	/shee/	/sez/	/cum/
	you	**comes**	**some**
	/yoo/	/cums/	/sum/
			snooze
			/snooz/

The Cat

and the Mouse

'No, no, no – look at that !' says the cat.

'My food is <u>gone</u>!'

Soon - Cat sees the cow.

'Did you take my food?' asks Cat.

1

'No. You <u>are</u> silly.

I like to eat grass', says Cow.

Cat sees the pig. <u>She</u> asks her,

'<u>What</u> about you?

Did you eat my food?'

2

'No, oink, no,' says Pig.

'It was not me.'

Brown mouse squeaks,

'I saw a big, black bird.'

Cat knows who it was now.

It was the crow!

3

The Cat and the Mouse

Page –	1	2	3
	gone	**are**	**was**
	/gon/	/ar/	/wuz/
		she	**knows**
		/shee/	/noze/
		what	**who**
		/wot/	/hoo/

The Dog

and the Farmer

The Dog and the Farmer

The dog wakes up and sees the crow.

He barks quite loudly and Crow flaps off.

Dog goes back to sleep.

He starts to snore.

1

In his dream

. . . he sees Crow stealing his food.

That wakes him up again. And <u>there</u> is the crow! She is eating from the cat's dish.

'Woof! Woof!' barks Dog.

2

The farmer comes out and sees what Crow is <u>doing</u>.

He takes the food inside the house.

Cat can eat her food inside now.

Later - she <u>lies</u> down with Dog and starts to purr.

3

The Dog and the Farmer

Page -	1	2	3
	goes	**there**	**doing**
	/goze/	/th e er/	/doo ing/
	snore		**lies**
	/snor/		/lize/

Making the Most of Your Child's Potential

Your child is now a reader! Congratulations on teaching your child one of the most important skills he or she will ever learn. You will have massively boosted your child's progress towards an especially bright, successful future.

To make the most of your efforts, try to find time to help your child practise his reading every day. Early reading books that contain a high concentration of words that are easy to sound out will produce the fastest progress. In addition, readers with a humorous element will boost your child's interest and enthusiasm towards reading. For a list of such books click here: https://readrightaway.com/resources; then scroll down to find a list of *Recommended Early Readers*.

Thanks to you, your child is now going to benefit from the many positive spin-off effects that come from learning to read: https://readrightaway.com/benefits-of-reading.

In fact, your child now has the potential to attain reading and spelling levels of achievement that are truly astounding, up to several years beyond his peers. You can read about this here: https://readrightaway.com/special-kind-of-phonics.

By playing the science-based *Teach a Child to Read in One Week* games with your child you will have speeded the growth of important neural pathways in your child's brain: https://readrightaway.com/reading-and-the-brain.

A study of 1,890 identical twin pairs over 10 years has now found evidence that early reading ability improves IQ: https://readrightaway.com/benefits-of-reading.

I sincerely hope that you and your child had fun playing these games and are pleased with the results. If you would like to leave a positive review on Amazon, the Read Right Away team always truly appreciates it: https://www.amazon.com/product-reviews/1999966392/ref=cm_cr_arp_d_viewopt_sr?ie=UTF8&reviewerType=all_reviews&pageNumber=1&sortBy=recent&filterByStar=five_star#reviews-filter-bar

Appendix 1: Comic Mnemonic Games - Reminder Cards

Cut on the dotted lines below and use one of the reminder cards that follow when you and your child are viewing the Comic Mnemonic pictures and playing the Comic Mnemonic Games together.

Game 1 - Shifty Shapes

Read the story and discuss what is happening in the picture. Ask, 'What does the letter *look* like? Discuss the reason *why*. Ask, 'Can you find another letter in the picture that looks the same?' Ask, 'Can you point to the letters in the text that look the same?' Point to letters in the story text, and ask, 'Is this a - (say the sound of the focus letter)?' Your child answers yes or no. Praise each time.

Game 2 – A Sound Story

Read the story again and ask questions about the letter's *sound:* 'What *sound* does this letter make?' Ask WHY the letter makes the certain sound. Ask your child to make the sound in different voices. Praise enthusiastically.

Game 3 – Talking Letters

Read the story again. Point to examples of the letter in the picture and ask your child to make its sound several times. Pretend to be hard of hearing so you can ask your child to repeat the sound. Find examples of this letter shape on packaging or tins, or while you are out shopping, and ask 'Do you remember what sound this letter says?' Praise highly.

Game 4- Let's Clown Around

Read the story again, but this time you and your child can adopt the letter's shape and act out the letter's character. Together, be as silly as you can be. Don't forget to make the letter's sound in a suitable voice.

Game 5 – Song and Dance Routine

Give your child a lower case letter card. Have your child compare the letter to the one in the Comic Mnemonic picture. Ask, 'Does this letter look the same as the one in the picture?' Ask your child, 'Can you put the letter the right way up beside the letter in the picture?' Once your child does this correctly it becomes the signal to begin the *Song and Dance* routine. Together, chant or sing the rhyming story while your child makes the letter dance around.

Appendix 1: Comic Mnemonic Games - Reminder Card

Cut on the dotted lines below and use one of the reminder cards that follow when you and your child are viewing the Comic Mnemonic pictures and playing the Comic Mnemonic Games together.

Game 1 - Shifty Shapes

Read the story and discuss what is happening in the picture. Ask, 'What does the letter *look* like? Discuss the reason *why*. Ask, 'Can you find another letter in the picture that looks the same?' Ask, 'Can you point to the letters in the text that look the same?' Point to letters in the story text, and ask, 'Is this a - (say the sound of the focus letter)?' Your child answers yes or no. Praise each time.

Game 2 – A Sound Story

Read the story again and ask questions about the letter's *sound:* 'What *sound* does this letter make?' Ask WHY the letter makes the certain sound. Ask your child to make the sound in different voices. Praise enthusiastically.

Game 3 – Talking Letters

Read the story again. Point to examples of the letter in the picture and ask your child to make its sound several times. Pretend to be hard of hearing so you can ask your child to repeat the sound. Find examples of this letter shape on packaging or tins, or while you are out shopping, and ask 'Do you remember what sound this letter says?' Praise highly.

Game 4- Let's Clown Around

Read the story again, but this time you and your child can adopt the letter's shape and act out the letter's character. Together, be as silly as you can be. Don't forget to make the letter's sound in a suitable voice.

Game 5 – Song and Dance Routine

Give your child a lower case letter card. Have your child compare the letter to the one in the Comic Mnemonic picture. Ask, 'Does this letter look the same as the one in the picture?' Ask your child, 'Can you put the letter the right way up beside the letter in the picture?' Once your child does this correctly it becomes the signal to begin the *Song and Dance* routine. Together, chant or sing the rhyming story while your child makes the letter dance around.

Made in the USA
Las Vegas, NV
01 June 2023